Can Our Church Live?

Redeveloping Congregations in Decline

Alice Mann

Foreword by Anthony G. Pappas

An Alban Institute Publication

Library of Congress Catalog Card #99-69580
ISBN 1-56699-226-5

CONTENTS

FOREWORD

"What's a Little Church to *Do*?" The sermon title summarized the plight of the 15 elderly members of a historic New England church. They were gathered that beautiful autumn morning not only to worship God but also—later, after enjoying a home-cooked chowder luncheon—to decide their communal fate. The sermon which, the pastor confided to me later, was the hardest he had had to prepare in his 15-year tenure among these people, outlined the alternatives: close, merge, or hang on.

The merger option was soundly rejected. Two previous attempts had failed, and there was no suitable congregation in sight. The moderator of the congregation then read two letters from members who could not be present. One suggested a larger sign and the other a child-evangelism program in the nearby apartment complexes. The pastor suggested an advertising blitz and the pastor's wife a renewed effort to develop a Sunday school. It soon became clear that the hang-on option did not mean that the last person alive ought to turn off the lights, but rather that these aged and exhausted folk ought to strike off on some bold new initiatives. The little energy they had left spent itself in a chorus of "We've tried that; it's impossible; who could do that?"

After an hour of discussion the option to close was the only one still on the table.

This true story may be a bit extreme, but it certainly gives the flavor of the dire circumstances in which many of our mainline congregations find themselves on the threshold of the third millennium of Christianity. Our churches are smaller, weaker, older, and often poorer. Our mission has lost its passion, its direction; our congregations their vitality and attractiveness. How could this happen?

Certainly demographic realities are factors. People have moved away. "Our" people move away. Strangers—people with different skin color, different language or accent, different orientation to life—move in. Still, there has yet to be a human being born without spiritual needs. The church described above is located in one of the fastest-growing towns in its state. Demographics have not been friendly to mainline churches, but there is more to our demise than this.

A more powerful factor, I believe, is the loss of our first love. We have forgotten that our God is in the redemption business and that we ought to be about "our Father's business." We have instead built up a whole enterprise around the maintenance business. The church noted above has an immaculate building, tidy records, ordered worship, regular fellowship. All fine and commendable things, but unsullied by the chaos of sinners being transformed and babes in the faith blundering their way toward spiritual adulthood. Unless we reenter the redemption business, we will soon be out of business—period.

A third factor is our confusion about the difference between form and content. We have developed a style of worshipping and following God that feels right for us—Sunday morning worship, organ music, monological communication, passive/receptive posture, measured pace, standing committees, Robert's Rules of Order, and so forth. These ways of doing things are alien and uncomfortable to those around our churches. We place on ourselves—even when we understand the redemption mandate—an impossible burden. First, we must convert people to our style of life, our preferences, behaviors, and thought forms. And then we can introduce them to the life-changing power of the Gospel. Yeah, right. If we keep the power of the Gospel from becoming incarnate, made fleshly and visible, in the lives of those who need it, can we make any claim at all to be followers of the Incarnated One?

Let me suggest a fourth factor: brittleness. We have become stuck and inflexible. We have lost the sense of adventure in our faith life. We can no longer imagine new possibilities and adapt ourselves to them. In the sermon mentioned above, the pastor clearly acknowledged that the congregation had many fewer options open to them now than they had had 15 years ago. But 15 years earlier, things weren't desperate, so why bother to change? Now it has become too late for them. The New Testament describes Jesus as the pioneer of our faith. But we have become unwilling to follow him beyond our comfort zones.

I suppose one could go on enumerating factors that have resulted in our present predicament. Alice Mann aptly summarizes these various factors contributing to the loss of vitality in many of our churches. But unlike this foreword, she does not stop with an analysis of the problem. She boldly peers into the future and invites us to discern God's solution, a faithful future for the congregations we love. Can waning and dying congregations actually live again? Mann paints us a picture of cautious but energizing optimism.

At the center of Mann's approach is congregational spirituality. She asserts the radical idea that each congregation has a divine vocation. God has called each congregation to a particular identity and ministry. This vocation is not static and fixed. It evolves over time and circumstances, but it is central. Without this sense of God's purpose, all efforts at redeveloping congregations will amount to little more than managerial tinkering. But with a sense of this unrefusable divine invitation, congregations can astound themselves and be transformed.

Yet, Mann further asserts, this calling into God's promise cannot come about without some time spent in the wilderness. For Christ's congregations, a quick fix may be no fix at all. Live with the issues, counsels Mann. Face into the pain. Give the Spirit time and opportunity to brood in your midst. Many congregations spend years in avoidance and denial and so back themselves into death or jump to a solution that will not bear their weight. Being reformed in the Spirit's crucible is not quick or easy; it is simply necessary.

No gnostic, Mann irritatingly reminds us that our new, refound faith must be embodied in time and place, in our contexts. It would be nice if we could just live serenely with the Lord (or even better, with people just like us), but God calls us to live with the needy folk around us. God calls us to be leaven in our context. Yes, we have to be holy, but we also have to get down and dirty.

OK, OK, good old mainline folk are saying, We are sold, convinced, repentant, and so on, and so forth, but what exactly can we *do*? Inability to imagine new possibilities is one of the reasons we are where we are. So Mann sets us a table full of options for congregations seeking to develop a new and more faithful future. She does this both in theoretical terms and also by means of mini-case studies. Every reader will have her mind expanded and his soul lifted. Truly God has given us many possibilities. And new ones will be discerned as we dig up the talents that we have buried and learn to use them in response to the Spirit's direction.

Yes, the little congregation of 15 old and tired folk did vote to close, but they added an amendment to their motion. They invited the denominational minister who had worked with them most closely to form a group to whom they would leave their building and their endowment for the purpose of starting a brand-new ministry in this same old place. They were betting on resurrection. Like Moses, they would see the promised land only from afar. They knew they couldn't do the work to get there themselves. But they still believed that God could. I believe they will be blessed for this last act of faithfulness. But how much more blessed might they have been if earlier they had allowed God to do a new thing in their midst?

ANTHONY G. PAPPAS
Old Colony Area Minister
The American Baptist Churches of Massachusetts

Since you have opened this book, you probably find yourself worshipping in—or working with—a declining congregation. The first thing I want you to know is that you are not alone. Vast numbers of mainline congregations are experiencing the same dilemmas.

Second, I want you to know that I have been there too. During my 19 years in parish ministry as an Episcopal priest, I served four congregations in severe decline and tried to help them turn around—with mixed results. Over the past 25 years, I have also served as a consultant to many such churches and to the denominational leaders who worry about them.

Third, I'd like you to know that you can gain new perspective on your situation, discover new resources, and consider new alternatives. Even in the past few months, as I have been putting this material together, I have encountered many new ideas and methods. Whether you are reading this volume on your own, or using it as a workbook for group study, I hope you will end up with the feeling that you now have access to the help you need.

Finally, I want you to know that this book bears some resemblance to a personal journal—most of the stories come from churches I have worked with as a consultant or served as a pastor. That gives it, I hope, a "real-life" quality. But you will also notice that the examples do not add up to a balanced, sociological sample of all churches in decline.

My experiences are shaped partly by historical accident—most redevelopment pastors are probably male, but I have written about three outstanding women involved with this type of ministry who are parish clergy, and two others who are denominational executives. My work over the years has also been shaped by my own "social location." I come from an Irish-German, Roman Catholic family in the Philadelphia area; my siblings and I are the first generation on either side of my lineage to complete undergraduate or advanced degrees. My ministry journey has generally taken me into white or interracial, English-speaking congregations that would generally be described as "middle class." Many other important stories remain untold.

As you prepare to turn the page, I want to express my thanks to the congregations and leaders who contributed to this project. Many are named in the text and in the notes. Where the story is more delicate, people are referred to indirectly or are included in a fictionalized account of events. Several colleagues have been generous enough to read my drafts and to offer suggestions. Beth Ann Gaede has been a treasured editorial companion from start to finish. Thanks to all.

CHAPTER 1

What Is Redevelopment?

Nothing on earth lives forever. Perhaps creation could have unfolded otherwise, but it did not. No living organism goes on forever. Instead, life expresses itself in cycles of birth and death, emergence and decline. The persistence of a species is assured not by the preservation of an individual specimen but by the capacity of each generation to sow the seeds of the next.

Understanding Your Congregation's Life Cycle

Social organisms—including faith communities—differ from biological ones in that they may outlive their individual members; nevertheless, they manifest similar patterns of emergence and decline. Key stages in the life cycle of a congregation can be described initially as a developmental arc[1] (figure 1).

Birth

Congregations identify their birth moments in a variety of ways: for example, the evening a group of people decided to start a church, the first worship service, or the occasion of official recognition by their denominational body. These earliest moments in the congregation's story contain powerful bits of genetic information that will express themselves in the rest of the life cycle. I recall the rather dramatic story of a suburban church founded by members of a downtown congregation during a period of "white flight" from urban areas. Decades later, members of my own nearby congregation would comment to me that they had—on their first or second visit there—

Figure 1: Life Cycle of a Congregation

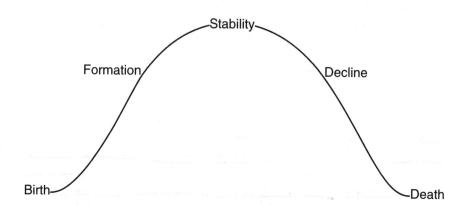

been told how awful the city was and why the church had moved to the suburbs. The fearfulness and alienation present at its moment of birth expressed itself in many other ways far into that church's life cycle. Though a new suburban ministry might have been needed to reach shifting populations at that moment, the negative tone of this congregation's founding impulse still resounded in the ears of every newcomer decades later, beyond the life span of most of the original members.

One vital piece of genetic coding has to do with size.[2] Those who study the planting of new churches have noticed how the number attending the first worship service "imprints" the congregation with a certain potential for natural growth. New churches tend to reach an attendance peak at five to ten times the number present at the first service, regardless of the population or receptivity of the surrounding community. Forty years ago, mainline congregations often started out with a dozen enthusiastic souls, only to level off with too few members for vital and sustainable ministry in their particular settings. Today's "church planters" are trained to spend a year or so organizing small home groups that never come together for public worship until critical mass can be reasonably assured.

Formation

The moment of birth gives way immediately to a period of formation, when the congregation's basic identity is established. During this time, the congregation develops its own tacit answers to three powerful questions:

Key {
1. Who are we (especially at a faith level)?
2. What are we here for?
3. Who is our neighbor?
}

In a "nation of immigrants," the religious identity of American congregations has often been shaped by cultural difference. Immigrant churches easily define "who we are," because "we" are noticeably different; our language, ethnicity, race, customs (or all of these) differ from the norm of the communities in which we have settled. "What we are here for" is also clear—to assure a transplanted people that our God is with us in this new (and perhaps inhospitable) place. Many Lutheran congregations, for example, were founded in the middle of the 19th century by German and Scandinavian populations arriving in America. Both their language and their sense of theological distinctiveness (forged in the crucible of European religious controversy) gave them a sharply defined identity within the American landscape.

Immigrant Church

Many congregations formed by past generations of immigrants can readily tell you when they stopped offering at least one service in the language and style of the "old country." Often this is a moment of identity crisis for the faith community, revolving around a painful question: "If we speak and dress and eat just like our neighbors, if our children have succeeded educationally and moved into the economic mainstream, why do we need our own congregation?" Lutheran churches founded in the colonial era were already losing their ethnic and confessional identity by the time those new waves of immigrants arrived in the 19th century. The ensuing conflict between proponents of Americanization and defenders of European-Lutheran particularity persisted for decades and shaped the character of Lutheranism in America.[3]

Even without a language difference, such an identity crisis can occur. In the late 1980s, I served a Trenton congregation that had been founded at the turn of the century by pottery workers from Stoke-upon-Trent, England. These immigrants, who had come to work in New Jersey's booming ceramic industry, built a small, neat church building a few blocks from one of the largest potteries. Nicknamed "cheeseheads" because of the cylindrical firing containers they carried on their heads—yellowish ceramic boxes resembling wheels of aged cheese—these workers merged successfully into the city's population and provided an education for their children. Their children's children came of age in the 1950s and 1960s, and moved out into the emerging suburban communities—a process accelerated by an outbreak of urban violence. The potteries eventually closed, along with much of the industrial base of the city; the church's neighborhood along a main route was transformed into a backwater by a highway bypass; and the remaining congregation dwindled, aged, and began to feel embattled. Their self-definition as an immigrant community at prayer had clearly run out of steam.

As congregations are born and develop, their answer to the third formative question—"Who is our neighbor?"—flows from the other two. If we understood ourselves at the beginning as an immigrant community at prayer, if our purpose was to "sing the Lord's song on foreign soil" in our own cultural idiom, then the neighbor on whom we focused our attention would be the household from our own cultural group. If, on the other hand, we started out as the "church around which the town was built" (a statement of historical identity by a Congregational church in a centuries-old community outside Boston), we would probably be accustomed to thinking of our neighbors as the whole town.

Both types of congregation may be facing a crisis today in the definition of "neighbor." The Trenton congregation, now surrounded by an extremely diverse mix of peoples, has been grappling with ways to relate itself to its fragmented environment. Could it minister to a newer immigrant group and function once again as an ethnic church? Could it develop a multicultural identity and attempt the hard work of building a place where cultures meet? Could it move five miles outside the city limits, where some of its old constituency still lives? Could it forge a clear identity around a distinctive style of worship and faith community that might draw people from a ten-mile radius? This church has chosen the last of these paths I have described, but it may have waited so long to make the transition that its resources will run out before the new reality can take root.

The congregation that helped to establish its historic Massachusetts town is also facing a crisis in its way of defining "neighbor." In the circle of communities just inside the Interstate 495 beltway, the strong identity of individual towns is giving way to a more regional reality. This church now draws members from the new housing developments constantly emerging in surrounding communities, a population more likely to be concerned about program quality and adequate parking than about the nuances of the town's history and politics. Many members have come and stayed because this congregation occupies a specific niche on the theological and political spectrum (they call themselves "open-minded") that may distinguish them from *Good* several surrounding churches of a similar tradition. The result of these internal and external forces is a crisis in defining self and other. Are we still the one, comprehensive Congregational church for neighbors in this one town? Or are we now a regional church, drawing people from a 10- to-15- mile suburban radius with our fine programs and our relatively liberal faith stance? What will our choice imply about the civic role of the congregation—our responsibility toward neighbors who are not members of this *Questions* church? Are we still, in any sense, a cornerstone institution in public life?

Stability *from Spiritual Development & Organization*

Ideally, the formative period in a congregation's life paves the way for a period of fruitful and sustainable ministry. Such stability has both institutional and spiritual dimensions that will, in the healthiest congregations, nourish and inform each other. When a congregation has forged a clear faith identity, and has organized its life to express that faith effectively and persistently within its community context, we might call that state "stability." *Key*

Sometimes only part of that equation is present. Many churches skip *2x* over the issues of spiritual formation early in their lives, devoting all their creative energy to the work of selecting a site, constructing buildings, paying off a mortgage, calling their clergy, and gaining ecclesiastical status as a "real" church. If the demographics are favorable and leaders make some unusually good judgments early on, this church might build a coherent spiritual identity around an effective long-term pastorate early in its life.

More often, the lack of priority given to faith development in the church's first years will leave an indelible imprint on its personality. Even the most able pastors may find themselves frustrated that money, buildings, and the togetherness of the founding group always seem to take priority over matters of ministry and spiritual formation. Perhaps the men who manage the investments rarely come to church. The women who painted the hall and sewed the curtains may not want smoky AA groups spoiling the interior.

None of these devoted leaders can understand why the pastor doesn't care more about them and give them more credit for their hard-won accomplishments. Nor can they understand why clergy are turning over so frequently, or getting into so many fights with a group of friendly people. A church like this may begin to grapple seriously with spiritual questions only after a major crisis provokes a soul-searching look at its own history and values.

Congregations may also come out of the formation phase with a clear faith identity but inadequate organization to live that faith effectively over time. For example, one of those churches that began with a dozen people at its first worship service may have become a spiritually vital congregation with aspirations of drawing many people from its community, but still find itself unequipped to navigate its first predictable size plateau. (Two-thirds of the American Baptist congregations planted in the 1950s, for example, hadn't broken through the 150-member mark by the 1960 denominational census.[4]) At first, the "glass ceiling" of a size plateau may provoke frustration and disappoint the outgoing spirit of the church. But if leaders can't diagnose the trouble as a common developmental crisis, the congregation will usually begin to rationalize its small size and denigrate ministries of invitation as "growth for growth's sake." At that point, an institutional crisis has damaged the congregation's soul.

If a congregation does attain both spiritual and institutional stability, it will always arrive at a moment when it is tempted to rest on its laurels, feeling that it has nothing more to learn except techniques for fine-tuning what already exists. As stagnation sets in, attendance and participation typically fall off, while membership and total giving continue to rise. Leaders commonly ignore or bury the earliest indications of decline and continue (with some strain) to focus on the positive. At this point in the life-cycle curve, congregations resemble the cartoon coyote who speeds off the edge of a cliff and keeps going straight ahead from sheer momentum—until he looks down and discovers there is nothing under his feet! Stagnation could be defined as the beginning of a decline we are not yet willing to acknowledge.

Decline

At some point, even the coyote realizes that he is falling. The congregation finds it can no longer dismiss as temporary or random the noticeable falloff in worship attendance, church-school registration, volunteer energy, pledging households, first-time visitors, new-member retention, and so on. After refusing for months, years, or even decades to "look down" at its situation, the congregation arrives at a moment of painful recognition.

Unfortunately, the most common reaction is blame. The board blames the pastor for letting fine old members drift or stomp away. The pastor blames the board for not leading the congregation in evangelism or tithing. Members blame their leaders, or the denomination, or the visitors who didn't return. Everyone blames the surrounding community and the wider culture for changing in ways that have threatened the congregation's survival. While there may be at least a kernel of truth in all these accusations, a blaming response is likely to accelerate the decline. Few people wish to join, attend, or lead an angry, depressed congregation.

Because congregations often feel helpless about changes in the external context, they are likely to focus their attention on matters they feel they can control: selling more clothing in their thrift shop, pressing the pastor for monthly reports on the number of visits made, resisting changes in worship that might upset well-established members. Little energy is devoted to fresh learning about the surrounding community, where fewer and fewer members may actually live as time goes by. Decisions are made by a shrinking core group of long-tenured members.

Death

If a congregation never replaces the blame response with a learning stance, or if it waits too long to try something new, death is the likely result. But death does not come easily. Denial and blame, the same responses that allowed the decline to continue unabated for decades, become the enemies of a holy death. Just as physicians and families once avoided the word "cancer" at all costs, many severely diminished congregations do not speak openly about the prospect that they may soon have to close. If a visiting denominational official raises this possibility, the church may have a sudden surge of energy to fight the outside threat, but that kind of activity rarely makes a difference to the church's basic viability.

This stage in the life cycle can drag on for a long time. I recently listened to the story of a 30-year-old congregation that had been founded and supported financially from the national level as part of a denominational church-planting program. After ten years, the denomination's mission department realized that early demographic projections had overestimated the opportunity in this location; the agency terminated the subsidy with the intention that the congregation would close. How did the church react? "They can't close us!" The congregation vowed to use its own modest resources to keep up the mortgage payments and to employ a pastor, creating a budget that was the institutional equivalent of a starvation diet. One leader spent her time collecting drippings from the altar candles and forming the wax around new strings so that the purchase of candles could be avoided. Until they had paid off the mortgage and proved they could survive, members would not consider the possibility of closing or merging.

Sometimes a congregation dies because it has completed its task, or because a changed environment is now calling forth an entirely different, kind of ministry. What would constitute a holy death in such a situation? The hospice movement has helped many individuals to make their last months both dignified and emotionally rich, but this cannot happen if the person keeps waiting for a cure. When a congregation faces its impending death sooner, while there are still enough members around for a wonderful "funeral" event, the concluding days of that faith community can be spiritually powerful. Bestowing a financial legacy on some other ministry that carries forward the congregation's values can provide an additional sense of self-esteem and continuity.

---

1. Take a moment to think about your own congregation. Where on the arc is your church today?

2. What clues or measurements did you rely upon as you answered question 1?

The Redevelopment Loop

Sometimes a terminally ill person will risk trying an experimental treatment—a radical and somewhat unpredictable intervention that could conceivably offer a new lease on life. Similarly, some courageous congregations facing serious decline attempt the difficult path of redevelopment, which involves:

- Recognizing the death of the congregation's previous identity and purpose.
- Reallocating the bulk of the congregation's resources to discovering and living out a new identity and purpose.
- Finding and empowering leaders who can, in effect, start a new congregation on an existing site.
- Caring for the remaining members of the previous congregation—sometimes by providing a separate chaplaincy ministry as long as it may be needed.

The redevelopment congregation finds substantially new answers to the three formation questions: Who are we? What are we here for? Who is our neighbor? Let's return to the life-cycle chart, to see where the redevelopment loop fits in (figure 2).

Figure 2: Renewal, Revitalization, Redevelopment

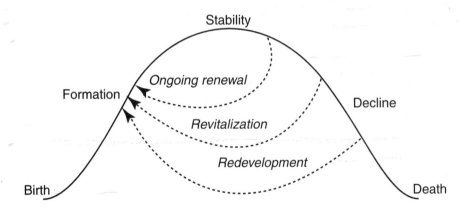

This chart shows loops back to the formation stage from three different points in the life cycle.

Ongoing Renewal

In a time when stability is drifting toward stagnation, a congregation might find a way to take a fresh look at the three formation questions. In the evangelical tradition, periodic revivals may have served this purpose to some extent, long before anyone started to study congregational development; in more catholic traditions, teams from religious orders would come to a church and conduct a preaching mission. These periods of intense proclamation, prayer, song, and study would interrupt "business as usual" and press the church back to fundamental questions of faith. Because they were system-wide interventions, they introduced common language and frameworks to which leaders could later refer as church decisions were made. Today it is common for churches to engage in strategic planning—even in times of relative stability—to refocus the congregation on fundamentals and to ask challenging questions about identity, purpose, and context. Other congregations rely on the self-study process that accompanies the selection of a new pastor to help them take stock.

Two tendencies prevent churches from revisiting the formation questions when everything seems to be working. First, the renewal event, self-study, or planning process may be rejected outright under the banner, "If it ain't broke, don't fix it." The new perspective provided by a revival leader, consultant, or self-study process may seem quite unnecessary, since the congregation's key programs are humming along successfully. Second, the congregation may undertake the process but discount any disturbing trends or hard questions that come to the surface. Some theorists argue that a system will never question its fundamental assumptions until the pain induced by present practices becomes intolerable.

Revitalization

In the early stages of decline, a congregation might gain some motivation to revisit the formation issues. If some way is found to look hard at the facts, avoid blame, and engage in new learning, we might call this process revitalization—a term implying that there is still substantial vitality present that can be refreshed and refocused. Though congregations usually expect that the call (or appointment) of a new pastor will accomplish this work automatically, a change in leadership will not, by itself, alter the curve. If the new pastor has the skills, information, and political support to raise the formation questions again effectively, a new era of vitality might ensue. More typically, the forces driving the decline—internal dysfunction, external change, or both—will be ignored until things get worse. In that case, the new pastor will experience (and often collude with) the congregation's two most destructive illusions: the fantasy that growth can occur without change, and the fantasy that change can occur without conflict.

Redevelopment

When a congregation has been declining steadily for years and even decades, when it has sustained significant losses in people, energy, flexibility, and funds, then the path back to the formation questions is far more costly. The farther you slip down the decline side of the curve, the more capital it takes—spiritually, financially, and politically—to create the possibility of a turnaround. Yet there may still be tremendous potential for spiritual growth, invitational outreach, and community ministry.

---

1. To what extent is your congregation now in the process of re-examining the three "formation" questions? By what means is that exploration taking place?

2. Is your congregation traveling on one of the three loops back to formation shown on the chart? Which one?

3. How far along are you in the journey toward a renewed identity and purpose?

In my experience, redevelopment efforts are often "undercapitalized" in all three ways. Many are set up for:

- *Spiritual failure*: The congregation has not really faced the fact that it is dying—that most elements of an old identity and purpose must be relinquished if anything new is to occur.

- *Financial failure*: Leaders are working with an inadequate budget or overoptimistic revenue projections.
- *Political stalemate*: Leaders—at both the congregational and denominational levels—severely underestimate the amount of political resistance that redevelopment efforts can provoke.

Those are stark assertions. I have presented them not to discourage the work of redevelopment—which has occupied a great deal of my ministry—but to increase the chances that specific redevelopment efforts will succeed. Redeveloping congregations are important to the whole church for several reasons:

- Often they are located in communities where the needs for ministry are enormous.
- Since all congregations will eventually face similar issues, these churches are engaged in important learning.
- Whether or not they succeed in establishing a new era of stability, redeveloping congregations live out the mystery of death and resurrection by "losing their life to find it."

Mike Regele has said it well in his book *Death of the Church*.[5] "The Church has a choice: to die as a result of its resistance to change or to die in order to live."

I hope that the rest of this volume will provide you with practical help as you assess where your congregation is today, and as you formulate a faithful response.

CHAPTER 2

Why Your Congregation
Is in Trouble Now

Congregations are born from a spark of interaction between faith and context. If you go back and review the founding story of your church, you will almost certainly discover that its emergence was closely linked with the political, economic, social, and religious dynamics of its wider community at a particular moment.

What Has Happened Outside Your Church

I have already noted this connection between faith and context in the Trenton congregation formed by English pottery workers seeking the employment opportunities of the Industrial Revolution, and in the Massachusetts church whose roots in the Puritan theocracy made it the central institution around which its town was founded. Here are other brief examples of such connection:

- In 1794, when St. George's Methodist Church in Philadelphia tried to segregate free black members, Absalom Jones and Richard Allen established two new congregations—St. Thomas' African Episcopal Church and Bethel Chapel African Methodist Episcopal Church (mother church of the AME denomination.)[1]
- Some former mill towns in the Northeast have two congregations of the same denomination—one founded for the owners and their social peers, and one designed originally for the mill workers.
- After World War II, the emergence of suburban developments around the major cities created a geographical and spiritual separation between home and work, between the personal and public realms. The

newly invented suburban congregation was expected to specialize in the family and personal dimensions of faith.

As we have seen, the founding impulse influences a congregation's identity, purpose, and outreach throughout its arc of development.

In periods of slow cultural change, the niche a church occupied within its community's ecology could remain constant for long periods of time. But, especially since World War II, the pace of change has accelerated in even the smallest towns, creating a growing gap between the congregation's original identity and present community realities. As you try to understand the decline your church has experienced, pause to ponder these questions:

1. Think about the "spark of interaction between faith and context" at the moment your congregation was founded. To what cultural realities did your church respond at its birth? (Think about both your local community and wider societal trends.)

2. Think about the "glory days" of your congregation. To what cultural realities was your church responding then?

3. What about today? What current cultural factors must your congregation come to terms with to frame a vital ministry?

Let's look at some broad cultural trends. After World War II, three enormous changes in American society converged: the baby boom, the emergence of the "automobile suburbs,"[2] and the Great Migration of African-Americans into the northern cities (a shift that had been in progress since the beginning of the 20th century). The suburban population, mainly white, doubled between 1950 and 1970.[3] During that same period, the total population of the United States increased by one-third—a net gain of about 50 million people.

Membership in most mainline denominations grew rapidly with the population until about 1965,[4] when the curve turned sharply downward. Here is a chart of combined membership in five U.S. Protestant groups: Presbyterian (U.S.A.), Episcopal, United Church of Christ, United Methodist, and Evangelical Lutheran (ELCA):[5]

Figure 3: Combined Membership in Five Mainline Denominations
(in millions)

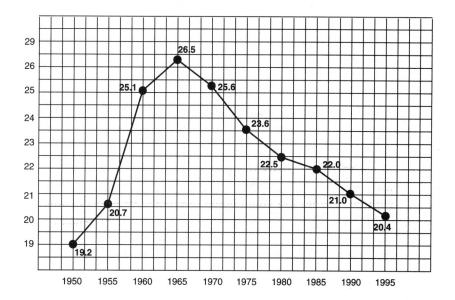

Though the details would vary for individual denominations, the overall shape of the chart would look somewhat similar to this one for any of the five. The downturn looks far more drastic when one notes that the total U.S. population continued a steep increase throughout this 50-year period.

Use the blank chart provided on the next page to graph your own church's trends in membership (or better still, annual averages of Sunday attendance) since 1950.

Figure 4: Membership (or Attendance) for
Your Congregation Since 1950

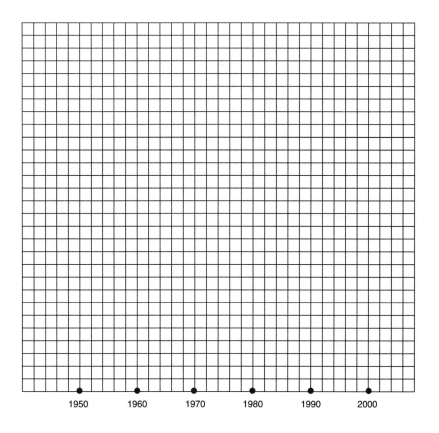

1950   1960   1970   1980   1990   2000

1. In what ways does the shape of your congregation's chart resemble the graph for five denominations? How does it differ?

2. Which of these "three enormous changes" affected your congregation's life? How?
    a) Postwar baby boom
    b) Emergence of the automobile suburbs
    c) Great Migration of African-Americans into northern cities

3. What feelings and thoughts do you have about the period(s) of decline on your chart?

What happened from the mid-1960s onward that reversed the fortunes of so many mainline congregations? During this era, the whole society experienced a series of upheavals.

*   Increasing intensity and visibility of civil rights protests
*   The assassinations of John F. Kennedy, Martin Luther King, Jr., and Robert F. Kennedy
*   Urban violence related to racial injustice
*   Escalating conflict over U.S. involvement in Vietnam
*   Increasing ethnic and religious diversity due to changed immigration laws[6]
*   Beginnings of the women's movement and the sexual revolution

Late wartime babies and early boomers approached adulthood at a crisis moment for key institutions. At first, that crisis affirmed the transformative power of religious faith—civil-rights protesters of the early 1960s exercised the powerful spiritual disciplines of nonviolent direct action; their disobedience was an assertion of hope for civic transformation. By the late '60s and early '70s, troubling events like the assassination of Dr. King provoked intense cynicism about public life—a change sealed and symbolized by the Watergate scandal. The dictum "Don't trust anyone over 30" applied to religious as well as secular authority, and the phrase "organized religion" became a derogatory remark.

As they reached "20-something," the church-school children of the 1950s did not reconnect with mainline congregations to nearly the extent that previous generations had. One factor was the postponement of marriage and childbearing—traditional triggers for renewed religious involvement. But even those starting families were not as likely to return to mainline congregations. By and large, they had not switched over to conservative or fundamentalist churches, as some claimed. Nor had they quit in anger over denominational programs or local-church style.[7] A more troubling explanation for their absence has emerged from careful research.

Those who had lost connection simply didn't see church participation as important any more. While members worrying about the decline wanted to know what they (or their denominations) were doing wrong, the engine driving this change had far less to do with church programs than with the "character of the culture surrounding the congregations."[8] This new context has been named the "marginalization of Christianity" or the "end of Christendom."[9]

The wave of societal enthusiasm for family-oriented religion, which had deposited people on the doorsteps of our churches in the 1950s, probably marked the end of an era of privilege for Christianity in North America. One Canadian theologian calls us to recognize "the effective disestablishment of the Christian religion in the Western world by secular, political, and alternative religious forces."[10] Didn't that disestablishment happen hundreds of years ago when the Constitution separated church from state? Yes, but only on the political level;[11] culturally, Protestant Christianity was still accepted as a social norm. A second disestablishment—this time of a religious type—occurred when the Roman Catholic and Jewish communities in America gained equal recognition as influences on American life. When I was in college, the standard sociology text on religion was Will Herberg's *Protestant, Catholic, Jew*. A third era of change—the *cultural* disestablishment of the whole Judeo-Christian tradition—is the one that suddenly became visible as the baby-boom generation reached adulthood.

As a result of this long and gradual shift in American attitudes toward religion, Christian congregations can no longer rely on the culture to inculcate biblical values or to promote commitment to local faith communities. While assent to rudimentary Christian beliefs is still common, religious pollster George Gallup has identified three gaps:[12]

- *An ethics gap.* People generally disconnect who they are (e.g., "an honest person") from what they do (what they report on their tax forms);

perhaps only one person in ten has a faith that makes a pervasive and visible difference in his or her life.[13]

- *A knowledge gap.* Many of those who assent to Christian doctrines like the divinity of Jesus lack even the simplest knowledge of the biblical story or other aspects of their faith tradition.
- *A gap between believing and belonging:* Americans view religion as a purely individual matter, and do not see "congregating" as an integral expression of faith. This attitude is held by church attenders almost as strongly as by the unchurched.

In short, the implications of religious faith do not penetrate very deeply into the soil of most people's lives, and the culture is rapidly withdrawing its tacit support for Christianity. The youngest generations of Americans may soon not even understand the questions religious pollsters have routinely asked. Imagine the exchange on the telephone: "Jesus who? Son of what?"

While many other changes are occurring in our wider context (see appendix A for a discussion of other trends identified by the Alban Institute), the most powerful event happening outside your church may be the end of Christianity's position as a culturally established religion. Some see this as bad news to be fixed, but I would encourage you to see it as an opportunity to clarify your congregation's identity, purpose, and outreach.

---

1. "The disestablishment of Christian religion" is more apparent in some regions of the country, and in some cultural groups, than in others. What signs do you see in your local community that support or refute the change described in this section?

2. Suppose it is true that the society will never again deliver people to your doorstep in the way it did in the 1950s—when all a church had to do was open the doors. What would this new situation require of your congregation?

3. How well is your congregation equipped to present the fundamentals of Christian faith and practice from scratch, to people with no prior knowledge at all? To people with negative attitudes toward Christianity?

To consider the impact of the external context—both wider culture and features of the local community—on the life of a congregation, let's look at the example of First Congregational Church of Waverley. Located in the town of Belmont, Massachusetts, First Congregational is preparing to call a minister who could be its last. Leaders are weighing the prospects for launching a new type of ministry on their current site with their remaining endowment fund of $500,000.

Belmont[14] is an almost entirely residential community about seven miles west of Boston and less than three miles from Harvard University. Until the construction of a railroad line in the 1840s, the local economy was based on agriculture and ice-cutting. Settlements grew up around the railway stations and attracted affluent Bostonians. The current town's territory was carved out of several adjoining towns in 1859, after a struggle underwritten by one wealthy merchant, who specified that the town should be named after his estate. The town grew quickly after a transit line connected the area with Harvard in 1912. Artists, authors, educators, physicians, and scientists moved in throughout the 20th century, especially to sections of town with old trees and larger homes. The population of Belmont peaked in the 1950s.

Waverley Square, located near the southern boundary of the town along a heavily traveled route, has over time developed a more urban atmosphere than other parts of Belmont. Its dense, modest housing has attracted somewhat less-affluent working families and individuals. This section adjoins the large campus of McLean Hospital, and subsidized housing is located nearby. Members observe that the area has drawn "Roman Catholics, French Canadians, and big families."

What is happening in the church's overall community context today? While the towns encircling Boston are still governed separately, they function as elements in a dense urban mosaic. The three-mile radius around First Congregational Church[15] overlaps several towns and constitutes the fourth-densest population center in the state (70,000 households). Eleven other United Church of Christ congregations lie within that circle, along with dozens of other churches. Compared to the U.S. average, the church's area contains:

- A highly educated and affluent population with little racial diversity
- A heavy concentration of people from 25 to 44 years old
- Far more single adults and markedly fewer children
- More people over 70
- More renters

The sharp rise in apartment rents around Boston is putting special pressure on the working-class population, who constitute perhaps a tenth of the total number living within the three-mile radius.

Members describe the current Waverley Square business district as "dead"—"ready for gentrification, but it's not happening." Except for the bakeshop, the neighborhood-oriented small businesses are gone. Right across the street from the church, several of the small storefronts have been joined into one large, busy bicycle shop, which serves both sports-minded cyclists in the region and people who commute on two wheels. Church leaders also point out that Waverley Square has many "special people"—developmentally impaired adults from the Fernald School and people receiving outpatient psychiatric treatment at McLean Hospital.

---

1. Imagine that you are helping this congregation to think about its future ministry. Which of the local community factors described in this section strike you as most significant?

2. Do you think that the "cultural disestablishment of Christianity" affects life in this community? How?

3. What information do you think these church leaders should gather about their surrounding community to reframe their ministry for a new era?

4. How would you feel if you were on the board?

We've begun this chapter by looking at changes in the wider culture and local community because they are probably the most powerful contributors to the ebb and flow of a congregation's life—accounting for 60 percent or more of numerical growth and decline.[16] Because these trends are so much bigger and more powerful than the individual faith community, we often don't know what to do with them. Confusion and powerlessness are uncomfortable feelings to acknowledge; it is generally easier to focus all our attention internally, on our own leaders and programs. What we do inside the congregation does, of course, make a difference. But if decisions about program, leadership, and finance are not based on a clear reading of the external environment, they will probably fail to advance the church's vitality.

What Has Happened Inside Your Congregation

Let's turn now to those internal characteristics that affect the development of a congregation. One of the most powerful is the way the congregation connects ends and means. Vital organizations[17] tend to be clear and persistent (even stubborn!) about their fundamental reason for being but flexible about the means they employ to live out their particular calling. A nonchurch example may be illuminating here. Some years ago, I consulted with the Association for Children in New Jersey. They were the successor body of an older organization, formed in the days when orphanages were the primary means for sheltering children who had no one else to care for them. As concepts about social services for children began to change, this association of orphanages faced a crisis. Had time passed it by?

Fortunately, this organization thought hard about its reason for being. In one sense, it existed to run orphanages. But why? What were the orphanages supposed to accomplish? What central values drove people to work so hard to provide those sheltering institutions? They began to articulate their deeper calling to protect and nurture children whose families could not do the whole job.

By articulating a more fundamental purpose than "running orphanages," they came to realize that their work wasn't finished. But they would have to get out of the orphanage business to continue that work in a changed environment. They sold all their properties (now valuable land for suburban development), created an enormous endowment fund, and went into an entirely different business—advocacy for the needs of children, especially those facing poverty, abuse, homelessness, and other traumatic circumstances. At the time I worked with ACNJ, its endowment income was sufficient to fund the entire operating expense of an influential agency lobbying statewide for the interests of children.

Let me use this story to make a distinction. In the first chapter, I said that redevelopment ministry begins when a congregation recognizes the death of its old identity and purpose. The ACNJ example can help us make a more subtle statement. Association leaders didn't leave behind *everything* from the past. But they had to distill that history down to one essential and persistent vocation, and then stand willing to change *everything else* to see that the core vocation continued. I wasn't around when they did that work, but I'll bet it felt like death.

Just imagine what they must have relinquished. The original donor families, who may have given their own land as orphanage sites, saw the properties sold. Buildings were razed that had been named after important leaders in the organization's past. Annual fund-raising events on the grounds of each institution came to an end, and hundreds of volunteers lost the meaning they had gained from assuming a helping role. Dozens of staff members running the orphanages had to be terminated. Children had to be moved out into other settings. And decision-makers had to take a risk on newer methods for providing social services to children—whichever way they decided, the caring leaders of ACNJ could have been criticized for making a wrong judgment about the well-being of the children themselves.

The central, hidden germ of identity and purpose didn't die; that seed was carried to a new patch of ground where it sprouted into a new and vital organism. But the parent organism did die in the process. The orphanages closed, and a whole new organization emerged to pursue the same fundamental vocation by dramatically different means.

---

1. Think about the story of ACNJ. What do you find exciting about its story? What do you find troubling?

2. What analogies might you draw between this secular organization and your own church?

3. ACNJ treated its core vocation as a "pearl of great price." Its leaders were literally willing to "sell everything they had" to exercise that vocation well in a dramatically changed environment. What is the core vocation of your congregation—the one you would "pay any price" to pursue?

Churches often reverse the prescription for vitality: They are doggedly persistent about means and fuzzy about ends. This is partly the result of our Christendom experience. When mission was "over there" somewhere, at the frontiers of a Christian empire, the congregation's role was to send financial support and the occasional young recruit. Inquiring into the mission of a particular congregation would have seemed as odd as asking someone, "What is the purpose of your town?"

A congregation's propensity to persist with familiar means may also be rooted in the nature of our human encounter with the holy: Ritual is fundamental to the religious experience. We might define congregational rituals as sacred actions, repeated with care and handed on through the generations. They may be elaborate ceremonies (High Mass or Bar Mitzvah) or simple gestures (reading from a large Bible on the lectern). They may be formal (bowing one's head when the minister says, "Let us pray") or informal (switching on the electric star over the crèche during the singing of "Silent Night" each Christmas Eve). They may take place when the community is gathered (singing hymns at a potluck supper), or people may be taught to use them at home (grace before meals).

The element of repetition is central. If we do not give ourselves over to a set of faith practices—suspending at least temporarily our desire to critique and control them—they will not help us to experience divine presence or spiritual transformation. I am intrigued to see how many of my neighbors show up year after year for classes in T'ai Chi, a set of ritual movements originating in a Taoist worldview and a theory of human integration (we might say "salvation") based on the movement of life energy. Many of these students are the unchurched baby boomers we spoke of before, seeking rituals that will center and heal their lives.

But rituals are also problematic. As both Protestant and Catholic reformers recognized, rituals often grow more stilted over time, more elaborate, and less transparent to the original faith experience they symbolized. Such traditions depend on periodic critique and renewal to retain their vitality. When we lose confidence in our most ancient and central faith rituals, when they become insipid or inconstant, we will invest our religious energies in the repetition of other patterns (innocuous enough in themselves) that contain little power to transform human lives or human communities.

I want to look again at the Trenton congregation founded by English pottery workers. They had brought with them some of the more negative features of 19th century Anglicanism, including a rather bland spirituality and a sense of shame about the outward expression of feelings (especially grief). When their priest's family lost a school-age child to cancer in the 1960s, the members mourned in a painfully private way; 20 years later, older parishioners still could not speak the word "cancer" in telling this story. During my tenure, a deeply beloved daughter of the congregation died in her 50s from breast cancer. While the newest members of the church were willing to go to her bedside to receive Holy Communion with her, the people who knew and loved her best declined to participate. One woman who had worked with her for decades on the altar guild explained, "I wouldn't know what to say to her."

While communion appeared to be the central ritual of the congregation, longtime members had not been formed in a sacramental devotion powerful enough to carry them past their fear of emotional exposure.[18] They could minister only vicariously through their priest, and even that link was tenuous—people would often go into the hospital for major surgery without letting the clergy know about it. Lacking a powerful personal connection with Word and Sacrament, members clung desperately to other patterns—especially customs related to remembrance of the dead. Fierce attention was paid to donor lists for memorial flowers and to the exact location of memorial objects.

---

1. What are some of your congregation's formal rituals? Which seem most central?

2. What are some of your congregation's informal rituals? Which of these would provoke the most conflict if neglected or changed?

3. Which of your congregation's rituals are most effective in providing courage to face times of chaos—illness, death, societal upheaval, church conflict?

4. You may want to pose the questions above to different subgroups in your congregation (people of a particular age, ethnicity, faith background, tenure in the church), and compare responses.

Though memorial gestures were valid expressions of people's piety (and silent grief), they were not robust enough rituals to fill the spiritual void carried forward from this congregation's early years.[19] During the formation stage, their self-definition as an immigrant community at prayer had not been undergirded by theological clarity (of the kind we noted in Lutheran immigrant churches); nor by a rich liturgical devotion (as one might have found in congregations of the Anglo-Catholic revival); nor by special zeal for social or evangelistic outreach. When it came time to dig deep for an underlying purpose (the way ACNJ did), this congregation found itself planted in a shallow bed.

For a congregation—a community powerfully shaped by the "means of grace" it has experienced—realigning means with ends is difficult work indeed. In spite of that difficulty, today's congregations must become articulate about their primary reason for being. Such clarity requires an honest look at behavior, not just rhetoric. Ed White, my colleague at the Alban Institute, has posed these questions[20] to church leaders:

- Is your congregation primarily in the *fellowship* business?
- Is your congregation primarily in the *social action* or *social service* business?
- Or is your congregation primarily in the business of *calling people into discipleship* and *forming them in a life-changing faith*?

I would add a few items to Ed White's list: Are you primarily in the *music* business? In the *historic preservation* business? In the *baby-sitting* business? In the *landlord* business? In the *investment management* business?

Any congregation will have a wide range of activities, some more central to its basic vocation than others. But it makes a dramatic difference when the "main thing" is clearly identified. I like the analogy of gathering stones from a riverbed into a jar. If you start by putting in a lot of little ones, the two or three big stones won't fit. But if you put in the "big things" first (the church's primary vocation, purpose, or mission), many smaller ones (supporting activities and minor projects) will find their proper place in the mix.

Lutheran researcher Alan Klaas raises the issue of purpose in a different way. Having directed a major review of internal factors affecting congregational vitality, he put attitudes toward outreach (both invitation and service) right at the top of the list. Regardless of size or social context, the churches most likely to grow: [21]

1) See themselves in mission beyond their current membership.
2) Have lay and clergy leadership which share that vision.
3) Are flexible in methods of communicating an unchanging message in a changing world.
4) Are action-oriented. They are not willing to be limited by challenges of size, language, availability of resources, or criticism by others.

A crucial element of a congregation's purpose is its answer to the question: Whom do we serve? When the primary answer is "our members," vitality is probably on the wane. On the other hand, when congregations focus on "being a missionary outpost in their community," they tend to draw new members even though "numerical growth is not their focus."[22] Klaas estimates that 20 to 30 percent of congregations demonstrate this kind of missionary vitality.

---

1. From your congregation's behavior, what primary "business" would you say your congregation actually pursues?

2. As you think about your congregation's central work, what are the two or three "big stones" that ought to go into the jar first?

3. If those aspects of your church's life were truly recognized as "the main things," what would have to be adjusted, decreased, or relinquished?

4. Is your church focused on meeting needs of current members, or on missionary outreach to your surrounding community?

A faith-based sense of purpose, one that draws us out beyond the walls of the church, is central to vitality. Now let's add a handful of other factors that emerge from decades of research about church growth and decline.[23] They are presented in the form of a self-assessment questionnaire that you can use individually or, even better, use and discuss with other leaders in your congregation.

Characteristics of Growing Churches[24]

1. A clear and positive identity

    This church conveys, in word and deed, a message that is truly "good news." We are known and respected in our community for our genuine strengths.

1	2	3	4	5	6
This doesn't describe us at all.			This describes us very well.		

2. Consistent focus on people who are not members

    While meeting members' needs, this church searches for ways to share faith within a changing world; to communicate with people not now active in our ministry; and to address real needs in our community through social action or social service. Both our pastor and our lay opinion leaders are outreach-oriented.

1	2	3	4	5	6
This doesn't describe us at all.			This describes us very well.		

3. Congregational harmony

    The way people interact with each other in this church lends credibility to our preaching and teaching. When differences arise, we address each other with openness and respect. We celebrate our shared life in many ways, and we are strong enough to face up to our failings as a community from time to time.

1	2	3	4	5	6
This doesn't describe us at all.			This describes us very well.		

4.   A positive dynamic between pastor and congregation

Our pastor brings real strengths to this church, and these are well-received by the congregation. We work to be clear and realistic about what we expect of each other. The relationship between pastor and congregation tends to foster trust and generate enthusiasm for ministry.

1	2	3	4	5	6
This doesn't describe us at all.			This describes us very well.		

5.   Small-group programming

We often form new small groups of various kinds, where people can know each other personally and relate their faith to daily life. We give special attention to the way such groups are formed, nurtured, and ended. We look for ways to involve in most of these groups people who are not currently members.

1	2	3	4	5	6
This doesn't describe us at all.			This describes us very well.		

© Alice Mann, The Alban Institute, Inc. 1996

How do these internal factors affect a congregation's vitality and its prospects for redevelopment? We will return to the example of First Congregational Church of Waverley.[25]

History and Key Personalities

The church's "birth moment" occurred in 1865, just six years after the town of Belmont was incorporated. A small group, meeting at the Waverley home of the Rev. J. W. Turner, decided to begin organizing a Congregational church. Later that year, 14 men and women formally launched the congregation and called Turner as their first minister. (He stayed for seven years.) With the laying of a cornerstone in 1869 on land donated by the Waverley Land Company, the church became the earliest place of worship erected in the Waverley precinct; it stands today as the oldest remaining church edifice in the town of Belmont.

Part of this church's founding impulse had to do with "getting there first" to meet both the expanding population and the swelling civic pride of a newly incorporated town. Comments in the church's historical documents provide a few other clues about its continuing relationship to its context. Two men raised in the congregation around the turn of the century had become town moderator and chair of Selectmen in Belmont by the time they addressed the church's 70th anniversary celebration in 1935—though the record suggests that they attended as products of the congregation rather than as current members. A powerful connection with academia is visible in descriptions of the dedication of Fellowship Hall (1953). The assembly was addressed by the president of Northeastern University (no doubt through the connections of a minister described below) on the theme "Makers of Civilization." While the text is not available to us, the title suggests to me profound confidence in Christendom.

The middle years of this congregation's life were marked by an unusual degree of clergy continuity. Two ministers in this century served tenures of 37 years—one from 1906 into the beginning of World War II, and the other, the Rev. Dr. Charles W. Havice, from the end of World War II through 1982. He was a distinguished academic, serving during his pastorate at First Congregational both as chairman of the Department of Philosophy and Religion at Northeastern University and as dean of chapel; he also held top leadership positions in a number of professional societies.

A beloved lay leader from Dr. Havice's era was Buddy Millett, director of religious education between 1950 and 1975. Here are some comments members made about this important figure in the spiritual life of the congregation:

"He was my mentor, and did that for many others, too."

"He always said, "You have to do it," preparing us to do things for
ourselves."
"He gave confidence, peace of mind; you knew you were doing
the right thing."
"Without Buddy, my son and daughter wouldn't have a religious
background."

Millet's sister—a vibrant older woman nicknamed "Ducky"—recalled with
fondness Buddy's bracing voice saying to her: "Rise above it, Ducky!"

Before we leave this era of the church's life, one other pattern might
be noted: Vocation to ordained ministry and full-time religious work has
been valued in this church. Historical documents recall with pride that First
Congregational has produced four candidates for the Congregational ministry, one lay professional, one missionary, and even one Episcopal bishop!

When the Rev. Paul Duhamel arrived in 1982, the church's life was
still cast in the mold of the 1950s. He initiated ministries geared to contemporary realities, such as a tough-love support group for parents who needed
guidance in crises with their children. (Several of the midlife adults in the
congregation today trace their spiritual commitment to that particular group.)
He served on the board of the Fernald School for developmentally impaired
adults, got members involved in cooking meals for a homeless shelter called
Bristol Lodge, and was known for his skill in crisis intervention.

Paul Duhamel is remembered as a person of "deep quiet faith," who
"never proselytized but let his work speak for him," and "touched many
people's lives." But during his ministry, the older generation continued to
miss the pastorate of Dr. Havice, the educational leadership of Buddy Millet, and the era of American life in which they had ministered. This nostal-
gia led to tensions which some identify as a major reason Duhamel shifted
to a full-time position directing volunteers at the Fernald School. Two subsequent pastors (both women) and a long-term interim have led a congregation in
steady decline marked by funerals, frictions, and the absence of newcomers.

Site and Buildings

First Congregational Church's building is located on a two-acre wedge
fronting on busy Trapelo Road, across a side street from the old brick fire
station. The church has more off-street parking than many city churches—
about 24 spaces—supplemented by on-street parking. The church is a modest

white-clapboard structure with an attached parish house on one side and a newer wing out the back containing an auditorium with a stage. Members take considerable pride in the small, healthy strip of lawn along the front of the church, newly restored through the installation of lawn sprinklers. As you climb the steps and walk through the main church door, you enter a high-ceilinged room, almost square, with dark-wood paneling and pews to seat about 100 people. The arrangement of the worship space has changed little since the church was built. Offices and a multipurpose living room are located half a flight down, with classrooms, auditorium, and kitchen another flight below.

Today's People and Programs

First Congregational today consists of about 30 active members, of whom five are Duhamels. Though Paul Duhamel did not continue to worship at Waverley when he left to work at the Fernald School, his family remained connected to the church. Today Paul's widow, Barbara, helps to anchor the small choir of women's voices; their son Tim, who works as a technical supervisor for a high-tech firm, serves as church moderator. Debbie, married to Tim, is a homemaker who until recently headed up the tiny church school (sometimes consisting only of their own two small children). About a dozen other adults between 35 and 55 make up the "working core" of the congregation—they feel overstretched trying to carry on the organizational tasks of a governing board, pastoral-relations committee, music committee, and search committee. Several have children who often do not attend, and one parent wonders if she shouldn't simply join a church with a functioning youth program. The church's older generation consists of about eight women who participate in a women's association, book club, Sunday worship, or all three.

Faithfully present for conversations about the parish's future has been Priscilla, a midlife adult suffering from mental illness, who speaks with simple eloquence about the importance of the church and its ministers as her anchoring community. Each week before church, Tim picks up two elderly women, Mary Louise and Mary, from the Waverley House (a group home for former Fernald School students). Four 12-step groups use the church facilities each week.

As part of their reflection process about the future, about a dozen members shared their favorite hymns and biblical stories. Reviewing their choices, members observed certain faith themes:

- An all-accepting God, caring for all "sorts and conditions" of people. ("When the woman washed Jesus' feet with her hair, he defended her for doing it. He defended me.")
- A present God, always there to be called upon. ("For me God was 'way up there,' so I asked for big bold letters to assure me of God's presence. A truck went by from the 'G.O.D.' trucking company, big bold letters; it woke me up!")
- A God who guides, comforts, helps, protects. ("He's with me, guides me.")
- A God who desires our response in good times as well as bad. ("Now I look to God, thanking him. Before, it was only in trouble or conflict.")
- A God who works miracles. ("How did he feed all those people? I believe he did.")
- A God who strengthens people to live through obstacles, and do things they thought were impossible. ("Noah was amazing, got all that lumber together on faith"; "What faith Joseph and Mary had!")

Some in the group were honest about their own religious struggles, seeing themselves as "doubting Thomases" in their hesitance to take things on faith, or as Peter denouncing Jesus—"Never say never; he did what he never thought he would do." Others noted how often their own connections with the church and with faith were rooted in the past, not the present. Yet another member commented: "We seem like a weary bunch!"

In relation to the choices they were preparing to make about a new minister and the church's future, they voiced these convictions:

- *We have to change.* Older members are dying off or tired; God is present now; the church will be here if God wants us here; God is in charge, not us; it's God's house.
- *We need to work together.* Some don't want to help at this time, but "Rise above it!" This is the day the Lord has made—rejoice and be glad; don't waste energy on what doesn't happen; some aren't called to do certain things; look to ourselves.
- *We need a bigger congregation to get more done.* We want a place of healing for older and younger people both.

The group also spent some time exploring negative aspects of their spiritual and communal life. These mainly revolved around themes of heavy obligation, leaders not feeling sufficiently authorized to do their tasks, and an atmosphere full of murmured criticism.

- "If Sunday School doesn't work, I feel like it's my fault"; "I feel I have to do this work—if I don't, it won't get done. That feels heavy."
- "The board empowered our committee to do something, then took a red pencil to it"; "We don't support each other in turmoil."
- "There's a lot of negative energy: apathy, criticism, and a 'telephone loop' [which undermines positive efforts]. In disagreement, people just leave or stop coming; there's a lot of murmuring."
- "We're ineffective at confrontation—we avoid it!"
- "We're dependent on the pastor; none of us feel adequate as facilitators."
- "We don't stick with our decisions—change too quickly if we hit bumps."
- "I don't really feel the sense of shared spirituality."

---

1. What are the key spiritual and material resources of this congregation today?

2. This church recognizes in itself many weaknesses. Which of these would you judge to be most crucial to address as it makes decisions about redevelopment?

3. Does any part of this church's story sound similar to yours?

For many congregations experiencing severe decline, unaddressed grief and depression rank high among the forces that block creative ministry. As you can see from the Belmont example, it is hard to relinquish an era of community and church vitality, a tight-knit circle of friends, or a beloved spiritual leader. The proper mourning of these cumulative losses in declining congregations tends to be short-circuited by:

- One or several remaining leaders taking undue responsibility to "keep the church open" or "make people happy."

- Denial of the changed circumstances, or magical optimism that the church's fortunes will reverse on their own (Alan Klaas has noted the latter tendency in his research).[26]
- An attitude of grim endurance, often underwritten by ever-increasing recourse to endowment funds to pay operating expenses.
- Seeking energy and unity through opposition to the denomination, or to any internal leader who may suggest a major change.

Whatever the mechanism of avoidance, one common factor is the absence of powerful rituals to mark and mourn the many losses people have experienced—not only in their church life but also in their civic and personal worlds. This "funeral" can never occur if there is no trusted figure who will solemnly "pronounce" the death of this church's past.

We have noted how silent and private grieving attached itself to remembrance rituals in the Trenton congregation. This same phenomenon was visible in another city church in the northeast, founded in the 1920s by families that played important roles in the city's commercial life. They had a grand vision for the main street of their city—a thriving and powerful church on the scale of a great cathedral. The women of this founding generation donated their jewelry to keep up mortgage payments during the Great Depression. When a beloved pastor died in the church's earlier years, his ashes were retained in the church building. The next generation of leaders (including sons of the founders) took this legacy upon their shoulders just as the city's economic fortunes were changing drastically. They felt a special responsibility to protect and manage the church's large endowment fund; in the congregation's informal parlance, these trustees were sometimes described as making "donations" to the church from "their" funds.

As happened in many other congregations (especially in the cities), the era of numerical decline beginning in the 1960s provoked anxiety, uncertainty, and conflict, along with some partially successful revitalization moves. But well into the 1990s, the "jewels and ashes" still symbolized dreams lost but not fully mourned. In the course of a long and difficult strategic-planning process, younger leaders (some in their 50s!) finally earned the respect of the "church fathers" and began to be treated as partners in church decision-making. The "telling of the history" at an all-parish gathering—including the stories of "jewels and ashes"—was a tense and pivotal moment in this transition process.

1. Among longer-tenured members of your congregation, what losses are still being mourned?

2. In what disguised forms does the grief express itself: stoic endurance, anger, depression, hopelessness, neglect of property, obsessive care of property, difficulty passing the mantle?

3. How might the losses be marked and mourned more overtly?

4. What trusted figures have the spiritual authority to "pronounce" the death of a past era, and so enable the expression of grief?

CHAPTER 3

Reconnecting Congregation with Context

If congregations are born from a spark of creative interaction between faith and context, can leaders rekindle such a spark later in a church's life? My answer is, "Yes, sometimes they can," because I have seen it happen. But it certainly isn't an easy process, especially after a long period of decline.

Tapping Hidden Energy

Consultant and educator Margaret Wheatley[1] has given us clues about how a new phase of "formation" might occur in a organization's life. Her eloquent book *Leadership and the New Science* challenges us to change the way we think about human systems. We are still burdened, she says, with a 17th-century view of the universe as an "exquisite machine"[2] whose creator set it in motion and then left the shop. This view, she argues, leaves us distrustful of life processes:

> Machines wear down; they eventually stop....This is a universe, we feel, that cannot be trusted with growth, rejuvenation, process. If we want progress, then we must provide the energy, the momentum, to reverse decay. By sheer force of will...we will make the world hang together. We will resist death.

As an alternative model, she describes scientific findings about self-renewing living systems (such as mature ecosystems, for example). According to Wheatley, self-renewing systems:

- Exchange information freely, both with the external environment and among the parts of the system; from this flow of information they draw the energy needed to counteract entropy.
- Change constantly, generating structures that fit the moment and relinquishing previous forms; they have a fluid quality.
- Maintain a discernible identity, rooted in the pattern of their own evolution. Their swirl of constant change is not random, but rather keeps them broadly consistent with their own history and identity.
- Show a remarkable resilience, or "global stability"; they can cope with—and sometimes even modify—fluctuations in their external environment.
- Allow their component parts a great deal of autonomy; they do not suppress small, internal disturbances by means of rigid central control.

In short, self-renewing living systems stay radically open to new information and change their shape constantly *in order to remain what they are.*

Let's apply those elements to congregations in decline. For regeneration to be possible at all, a congregation's "inside" has to start dancing again with its "outside" realities. Its internal components have to loosen up so that they can vibrate, bump into each other, collapse, multiply, and—most of all—communicate with each other. A new phase of life might be possible for your congregation to the extent that your leaders and members can:

- *Start learning together about the congregation and its environment.* "Who was that visitor, anyway?" "Why are our board meetings so depressing?" "Who bought the house down the block?" "Why did that business close?"
- *Let failing structures and styles collapse.* "We can't sustain a four-part choir, so let's do some other kind of music."
- *Retell the congregation's faith-story relentlessly until its essence becomes clear.* "What has been our distinctive contribution to the life of this community over the years? How could we pursue some faith-task in a totally different way?"
- *Embrace risks, mistakes, disagreements, even disasters as opportunities to trust God and to live your faith.* "Let's get together after our new worship service and talk about how it went—remember, we'll be feeling a little vulnerable!" "The city says our soup kitchen doesn't meet the codes; let's gather to pray and think about what to do next."

- *Accept the fact that your congregation may die no matter what you do.* As leaders in Belmont said: "The church will be here if God wants it here; God is in charge, not us."

---

1. What is your reaction to the five disciplines listed above?

2. Which ones does your church do best?

3. Which are most difficult for your congregation?

These redevelopment disciplines are based on an underlying faith that deep creative processes still move beneath our feet today.

I would identify that hidden creative energy as the Spirit of God, still blowing over the face of the waters and still bringing forth a whole universe—beautiful, chaotic, yet persistently manifesting the tendency toward order. In the equally mystical language of complexity theory, we might speak of *autopoiesis* (from the Greek for self-making): "The characteristic of living systems to continuously renew themselves and to regulate this process in such a way that the integrity of their structure is maintained."[3] Here, "maintaining structure" does not imply any rigidity of form; rather, this phrase refers to the persistent emergence of a signature pattern within the endless swirl of chaotic change. (If you watch the "Nova" series on television, you have probably seen this pattern-emerging-within-chaos illustrated by colorful computer-generated fractal images. A recognizable paisley design pops out, then dissolves, from moment to moment, as the computer zooms in to change scale.)

If you can tap into that creative energy again now, you will discover that there is some next step—toward a renewed life or toward a holy death—that can faithfully express the essence of your congregation's vocation within the realities of the historical moment. Chapter 4 will help you to consider some of the concrete alternatives. But first, let's try to understand why that creative energy seems so deeply buried now.

I would bet that in its early years, your congregation was radically open to external information—local demographics, wider cultural realities, and religious trends. How can I be so sure? Your church wouldn't be here today if it had not drawn significant energy from its environment. Think about the energies that engendered some of the congregations I have discussed so far:

- The wave of industrial energy that brought Anglican pottery workers together in Trenton to found a church.
- The wave of physical growth and civic self-consciousness in Belmont that powered the formation of First Congregational.
- The wave of commercial energy on a New England city's main street that spawned a massive Protestant cathedral during the "Roaring '20s."
- The wave of fear and anger that carried members of a city church to the suburbs in the 1960s.

Remember that a congregation may draw its energy either from flowing with or from fighting its context. The Bethel AME Church in colonial Philadelphia resisted the subordination of black Christians by creating a new, autonomous institution. In 19th century Anglicanism, both catholic and evangelical movements spawned congregations in rebellion against the bland spirituality of the mainstream. The second great wave of Lutheran immigrants rebelled against the Americanization they observed in their longer-established brothers and sisters.

One way or the other, a newly founded congregation brings faith and context together as partners in a complicated dance. Forms are fluid and innovative at the beginning: Congregations shape themselves to the exigencies of the moment, the same way a sapling shapes itself to reach the available light.

---

1. When your congregation was founded, would you say that it gained energy by "flowing with" or "fighting" the religious and social context? How?

2. What was true in the "glory days"?

3. What is happening today?

Regaining Flexibility

What happens after the spurt of founding energy? As the congregation gathers resources and takes shape, innovation typically drops off. Three charts below illustrate this relationship. Figure 5 shows what typically happens over time to a congregation's resources—people, energy, money, physical plant.

Figure 5: Total Congregational Resources (People, energy, money, buildings)

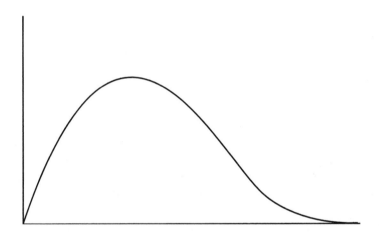

I have not shown a symmetrical arc. At least for mainline denominations (whose congregations quickly become elaborate institutions) the decline side of the cycle seems to last longer than the formation side. Toward the end, when most of the energy and people have disappeared, it may take years for someone finally to turn off the lights.

Figure 6 shows what happens to a congregation's willingness to innovate—its tolerance for change:

Figure 6: Congregation's Tolerance for Change

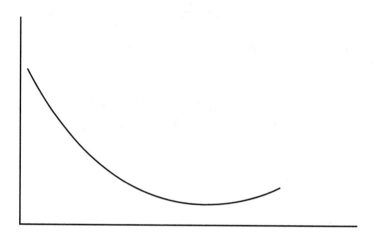

Congregations typically lose their visionary, entrepreneurial, and missionary qualities rather quickly. Once the founders begin assembling the people, buildings, leadership, and official status to approximate their concept of a "real" congregation (on whatever scale they have in mind), tolerance for change drops off quickly and may nearly disappear at the point of "success." Lay leaders and clergy stop thinking so much about reaching people outside their walls and instead focus inward. (While founding pastors tend to be entrepreneurial spirits, the congregation will often pick a successor to nurture the flock already assembled.) Boards start to focus on keeping current members happy.[4] It usually takes a great deal of decline to unsettle the status quo and to provoke a grudging admission that something has to change.

How do these two curves interact? Figure 7 shows the possible relationship between a congregation's total resources and its tolerance for change. When the steady drop in resources combines with a few incipient moves to try something different, the "chemistry" of the system produces a crisis—a moment of decision which Margaret Wheatley calls a "bifurcation point." "[At this] crossroads between death and transformation...the system encounters a future that is wide open. No one can predict which evolutionary path it will take."[5]

Figure 7: Total Resources and Change Tolerance

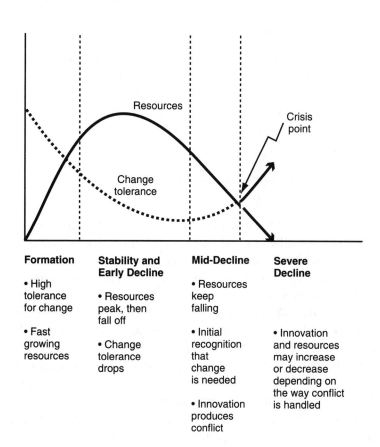

Formation	Stability and Early Decline	Mid-Decline	Severe Decline
• High tolerance for change	• Resources peak, then fall off	• Resources keep falling	
• Fast growing resources	• Change tolerance drops	• Initial recognition that change is needed	• Innovation and resources may increase or decrease depending on the way conflict is handled
		• Innovation produces conflict	

When the decline trajectory collides with the first tentative moves toward innovation, both energy and conflict are generated. On the other side of this intersection, the congregation's capacity for creative adaptation may bounce up (toward greater innovation) or down (shutting off discussion entirely, moving toward death in a state of persistent denial, anger, or depression).

---

1. Where would you say your congregation is located on the chart in figure 7?

2. Have you experienced one or more crisis points?

3. When and how?

The flash point sometimes occurs early in the tenure of a new pastor who has been called to "help the church grow." The pastor—who may be recently ordained and full of new ideas—doesn't realize that the growth mandate has a couple of footnotes attached. "We want you to bring in new people. But one, don't change anything important (and everything is important to *somebody*), and two, keep everyone happy (especially the pillars of the church)." As soon as the new pastor starts making changes, the unspoken parts of the mandate are violated.

Conflict ensues. Sometimes the issues are addressed well, and the congregation contracts with its pastor for an agreed-upon change agenda; more often, the pastoral relationship doesn't survive the crisis (the minister either leaves or becomes depressed and paralyzed), and the congregation burrows deeper into its old pattern. The crisis point can also be precipitated by lay leaders who "force the issue" of the congregation's decline onto the board agenda for some kind of action, as happened in the case of Holy Trinity Church, Jackson Harbor (a northeast resort community).[6]

After 25 years as a summer chapel for affluent urbanites, Holy Trinity was transformed into a year-round congregation in the early 1950s—largely through the efforts of a dynamic group of women who shared the vision of a "full-time church." As you read this congregation's published history, you notice immediately how one growth goal after another was achieved

between 1950 and 1970: establishing a year-round schedule, adding buildings and parking, securing full-time clergy leadership, achieving full status
within the denomination. The attendance peak came between 1965 and
1970; after that, the church proceeded down a curve almost the mirror
image of its 20 previous years. External factors were important in shaping
the arc of Holy Trinity's life. Though many new people kept moving to the
area as year-round residents, there were many new churches for them to
attend. And, as we have seen, mainline denominations experienced a broad
pattern of membership decline from 1965 onward.

But factors internal to this church's life were critically important to the
immediate decline it experienced. The congregation's attendance stopped
growing at exactly the moment it attained its vision—a year-round schedule with a full-time minister and a full complement of church buildings.
Members' boldness and energy seem to have died at that instant. You can
feel a dramatic change of tone in the written narrative when you reach
1970 or so. For one thing, the congregation suddenly started contributing to
an overseas project at that moment—right at the peak of its curve. While
wider mission involvement is generally a sign of health, here it also seemed
to underscore the absence of any further vision for local outreach. Nearly
all the innovations recorded from 1970 on were adjustments to numerical
decline. To meet the growing budget crunch, members started a thrift shop
and inaugurated a weekly craft fair to raise funds from summer tourists.
They downsized the choir program and scaled back their worship on principal holy days. Major volunteer energy went into building repairs.

This congregation clearly lost touch with the dynamics of its local
community as the years went on. By the middle of the 1970s, the advancing
age of the membership and the drop-off in attendance had become quite
noticeable (though the number of members on the official list kept increasing until it hit 400 by the 50th anniversary in 1976). As leaders tried to
interpret these changes, they cited a large national increase in the proportion of people over 65 as a possible explanation; perhaps Holy Trinity was
simply aging and declining along with the rest of the nation and the rest of
the community. This area does have a high concentration of retirees; but
when leaders studied a demographic profile a few years ago, they were
amazed to discover that 60 percent of the population within a ten-mile radius was under 55. Keep in mind that I am speaking of their *communal*
understanding of the context. Though individual board members possessed
information about growing schools and growing congregations all around

them, the leadership *group* was unable to weave this information into a realistic "story" about the church's context.

Not only did leaders have trouble processing information *from* the surrounding community; they were also sending little information out *into* their environment. In fact, the congregation had practically slipped off the community's radar screen. When a town planning official was interviewed about trends in the area, he could not at first recall where this church was located—even though it sits on a main route he traveled every day.

What precipitated the crisis? The top elected leader started pressing for some kind of external assessment of the situation, including the role of the pastor in the church's decline. Among other issues, this church officer was concerned about the amount of energy the pastor seemed to invest in his long-standing ministry at a battered-women's shelter—a project in which the congregation was not involved. As the confrontation heated up, emotional agitation increased between him and the pastor, who experienced some of this leader's behavior as controlling, critical, and manipulative. The pastor also perceived that the complaints brought forward were not widely shared in the congregation.

While many of the details are peculiar to Holy Trinity, some elements of this story are frequently found at the "crisis point" in figure 7:

- Emotional tension rises.
- One lay leader (or a small group) feels a special burden to "save" the congregation.
- A long-serving pastor's ministry comes under intense scrutiny (after many years, perhaps, with no structured evaluation at all), and the incumbent becomes defensive.
- The pastor resents the board's attempt to "change the contract" after years of accepting, even rewarding, a low-key, caretaker role (a reaction that grows in intensity as the pastor approaches retirement age).
- Most leaders become confused and feel pressured to choose sides.
- Help from outside (a denominational official or an independent consultant) is both desired and feared.

Holy Trinity did secure outside help in making a broad assessment of its situation. Despite some rocky patches at the beginning of the work, the congregation kept working with a consultant for about 18 months. One result was that the board negotiated a mutually acceptable early-retirement date with the pastor, creating a clear time frame in which lay

leaders could prepare for the pastor's departure and undertake some preliminary revitalization projects. Some of their early initiatives have generated new energy and raised the congregation's self-esteem—adding a few
fresh elements to worship, providing more support for their volunteer church-
school teacher, sprucing up the grounds and the church exterior. These
efforts also highlighted some long-term dynamics, including a lack of connection and teamwork among various parts of the system. Leaders have
stayed open to new learning over the past two years, and have generally
made use of setbacks to hone their skills for group problem-solving. They
may soon be able to enter a clergy search with some measure of realism
about the kinds of change that growth may require of them.

---

1. Look again at figure 7. Would you change your answer about
   where your congregation is on the chart? How?

2. If you have experienced one or more crisis points of the kind
   described on the chart, describe what precipitated them.

3. What new insights have you gained from the examples provided above?

Renewed Identity and Purpose

At this stage in its life, Holy Trinity has re-established a flow of accurate
information into and through the congregational system. The leadership circle
has gained some new suppleness and group strength by tackling several
modest goals together. The group may now be ready to start addressing the
big questions: Who are we at a faith level? What are we here for? Who is
our neighbor? This is exactly the same work that lies ahead for First Congregational, Belmont. Right now leaders are beginning these explorations
as they prepare to search for a new minister, but their wrestling with these
questions will probably continue for several years once that new minister
arrives. (Given the pace of change in our communities, congregations will
need to revisit these questions in a focused way at least once every five

years.) Perhaps this same work lies ahead for your church as well. What would be the elements of that exploration?

The chart (figure 8) on the following page maps out a pattern of elements that may begin to flow toward renewed identity and purpose for your church. In this process, the inner life of your congregation becomes connected in a fresh way to the world around you, through a process of discernment. While it is vitally important to recognize your church's weaknesses, and to identify the tough challenges in your social context, the heart of your work will be to discover a fresh connection between your congregation's strengths and the opportunities for ministry in your community today. That's why those boxes are central on the chart.

Figure 8:
Reconnecting Faith and Context

Congregation   **Local Community and
Wider Culture**

Strengths

Central faith-
themes distilled
from history

Present
resources:
spiritual, human,
material

Emerging or
potential
competencies
(may grow from
facing our
weaknesses)

Opportunities

Populations

Unmet spiritual
needs

Unmet
community
needs

Unfilled niches
in religious
ecology

Weaknesses

Key dynamics
and difficulties
that will
undermine
redevelopment
if not addressed

Challenges

Tough realities
in our context
that we must
face in order
to live out
our vocation
today

Discernment

Renewed Identity and Purpose

What is our enduring faith-task, and what fresh form could it take today?
What do we wish to be known for in our community?
To what size are we called to aspire now?
What is the quality of life we seek within the congregation?
What guiding story or image crystallizes our vocation?

Strengths and Weaknesses

If you filled out the five-point inventory in chapter 2 ("Characteristics of
Growing Churches Assessment," pp. 28-29), you have some initial information about your congregation's inner life. Because each of these five
items contains several sentences of definition, a group of leaders could
spend considerable time discussing their responses to the inventory. After
the discussion, you could summarize key strengths and weaknesses.

Any good church-planning model will provide you with other categories to reflect upon. If you are looking for a printed resource, I would recommend *Discerning Your Congregation's Future*, by Roy Oswald and
Bob Friedrich,[7] for three reasons. First, this guide sets the entire assessment task in the context of spiritual discernment; as we have noted, many
congregations enter the decline cycle partly because they are spiritually
malnourished. Second, the self-assessment method in this book goes beyond the usual programmatic "boxes" (worship, education, pastoral care,
etc.) to look for themes and meanings in a church's oral history, and to help
people catalog the norms ("unwritten rules") of their own congregation.
Undertaking fresh learning about your congregation's history and norms
will help you recognize deep currents—some creative, some problematic—
that shape the parish personality. New energy arises from storytelling and
truth-telling, when they are undertaken in a spirit of loving curiosity. Third, I
suggest this book because it offers specific group-process suggestions. For
many congregations far into decline, the full process described in the book
would be overwhelming and inappropriate. But because it is so specific, it can
provide you with sound ideas for shaping conversations that can release transforming energies. Overall, the process outlined in the book includes:

• Discernment and prayer—not as a separate step, but as a pervasive
  attitude and practice.
• Appointment of a task force.
• Assessment of the congregation's ministry using several different tools.
• Identification of the congregation's norms (habits, patterns, unwritten
  rules).
• Interviews with key people in the community.
• Development of prioritized goals, with involvement of both the congre-
  gation and the governing board.
• Development of a mission statement.

I recommend, as the book does, that you obtain the help of an outside consultant as you undertake this kind of review. Congregations far down the path of decline are usually out of practice with this kind of work. While you may be tempted to ask the pastor, a lay leader, or a committee to handle the process, know that this is unwise—in fact, refusing to seek outside help may be a pattern from the past that has gotten you into deep trouble before. Perhaps the most crucial strengths you will identify are the faith themes at the heart of your congregation's life. Carl Dudley and Sally Johnson[8] have gleaned from their study of congregational narratives five kinds of stories that shape ministry:

- Journey stories of ethnic-cultural congregations.
- Crisis stories of churches that struggle for survival.
- Rooted stories with a place for spiritual growth.
- Service stories of caring for people.
- Mission stories of vision for a better world.

After an evening of retelling your congregation's history together, you might ask if one of these story types fits your church.

---

1. When you think about the overall shape of your congregation's history and ethos, which of the five story types fits your church best?

2. How does that underlying narrative affect your church's thinking about redevelopment possibilities?

   Look again at figure 8. Note that I have included in the "strengths" box a place for emerging or potential capacities. Sometimes you will see just a glimmer of a competence that could be carefully nourished and developed. ("Gosh, Jane did a wonderful job preparing that child to read in church. I wonder if we could expand on that.") In other cases, you will see the *possibility* of gaining a competence that doesn't exist at all. ("Our local community organization trains people to do one-on-one interviews; we could

use that skill as we try to get more connected to our own members.")
Sometimes, a tragedy or trauma that seems to be a parish weakness will
turn into a central ministry strength. For example, if your congregation has
done the painful work of addressing sexual misconduct in your midst, you
have probably gained profoundly important strengths (truth-telling, admit-
ting mistakes, holding people accountable, compassionate listening). Such a
church might find it has a special capacity to minister to battered families or
some other segment of your community.

Take a moment to list some of your congregation's strengths:

1. Central faith themes

2. Current competencies

3. Spiritual, human, and material resources

4. Emerging or potential competencies (may grow from facing a
   weakness)

Opportunities and Challenges

On the right-hand side of the chart in figure 8, you will be exploring realities in your local community. Carl Dudley's fine book *Basic Steps in Community Ministry*[9] provides an outline of the work to be done—plus detailed steps and a wealth of true stories. To explore your social context, Dudley says, your congregation will need to undertake five tasks. I have placed a blank box under each item so that you can write down your initial ideas about content or process.

- *Define Your Community.* You can define your community from many perspectives, but we will focus on three: (a) chart the physical boundaries, (b) identify the anchor institutions, and (c) look for the gathering places.

> Initial thoughts

- *Identify the People.* I suggest three perspectives: (a) observe populations and lifestyles, (b) note historical changes and current trends, and (c) review statistical summaries.

> Initial thoughts

- *Find the "Invisible" People.* Every community has people who are ignored, marginalized, or simply out of sight. By identifying these groups, your committee and the congregation become more sensitive to a range of conditions in your community.

```
Initial thoughts




```

- *Analyze the Intangible Forces.* Just as churches have always been concerned with spiritual forces, you should identify the social, economic, political, and religious forces operating in your community. These forces may be intangible, but they are real incentives and barriers in the lives of the people you are trying to reach and in the development of your ministry.

```
Initial thoughts




```

- *Listen to Your Community.* Based on this wealth of data and feelings, you can initiate conversations with a wide varietyh of people from every segment of community life.

```
Initial thoughts




```

When you are ready to look at statistical information about your community, you may want to order a demographic profile from one of the companies that prepare them especially for religious congregations. A profile from the organization called Percept[10] will cost your church several hundred dollars (unless your denomination has an arrangement for obtaining this resource at a reduced cost.) I have found Percept's material far more focused and helpful than other statistical reports I have seen, but be warned: you will receive far more information than most people can possibly assimilate. I usually ask congregations to focus their attention on the "Snapshot" page, which summarizes critical information quite succinctly. Figure 9 shows a sample of such a page.

Figure 9: "Snapshot" Page from a Percept "Ministry Area Profile"

Snapshot

Coordinates: 42:23:02 71:11:79
Date: 6/11/99

Prepared For:
Massachusetts Conference UCC
ImagineArea #4
W. Cambridge, MA

Study Area Definition:
3.0 Mile Radius

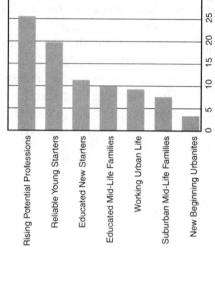

Primary U.S. Lifestyles Segments—1999

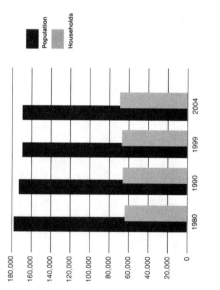

Populations and Households

The population in the study area has decreased by 4142 persons or 2.4% since 1990 and is projected to increase by 41 persons, or 0.0% between 1999 and 2004. The number of households has increased by 1009, or 1.5% since 1990 and is projected to increase by 1662, or 2.4% between 1999 and 2004.

Population by Race/Ethnicity Trend

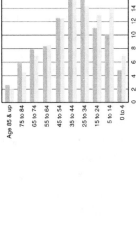

Population By Race/Ethnicity—1999

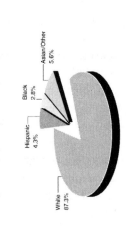

Between 1999 and 2004, the White population is projected to decrease by 4252 persons and to decrease from 87.3% to 84.7% of the total population. The Black population is projected to increase by 850 persons and to increase from 2.8% to 3.3% of the total. The Hispanic/Latino population is projected to increase by 1151 persons and to increase from 4.3% to 4.9% of the total. The Asian/Other population is projected to increase by 2292 persons and to increase from 5.6% to 7.0% of the total population

Population by Age—1999

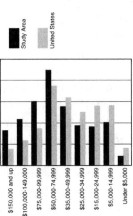

Households By Income—1999

The average household income in the study area is $69965 a year compared to the U.S average of $53198. The average age in the study area is 39.9 and is projected to increase to 40.8 by 2004. The average age in the U.S. is 36.5 and is projected to increase to 37.3 by 2004.

(800) 442-5277

© 1998-99 Percept Group, Inc.

Sources: Percept, National Decision Systems, U.S. Census Bureau

ID# 20338:6-543

A study group can work back from that "Snapshot" page into the extensive supporting material to answer particular questions the congregation may be pursuing. Figure 10 (on page 59) is a worksheet that I provide to a self-study team to use when the members are examining their Percept "Ministry Are Profile" (consisting of the "Snapshot" summary, plus the workbook of detailed supporting material).

One of the most important kinds of information you will get from a community. This information is located in figure 9 on pages 56 and 57. An extensive marketing database divides the U.S. population into 50 subcultures. "Lifestyle segment" is the technical name for one of these groups. As an example, look at a few of the lifestyle segments which Holy Trinity, Jackson Harbor, discovered within a ten-mile radius (as described in the members' own summary of their situation):

- "Established Empty Nesters" are located in the area along the lake. This demographic segment comprises one-third of the population within ten miles of the church. The younger end of this group (in their 40s and early 50s) needs special attention. Among other things, this group tends to look for spiritual retreats as part of a church program.

- "Urban Senior Life" are located at the northern edge of Jackson Harbor. Nationally, this group includes many Episcopalians. Adult theological discussion groups are among their expectations of a church. Current programming at Holy Trinity seems to match the needs of this segment most closely.

- "New Beginning Urbanites" are located from Jackson Harbor into the eastern edge of Brownsville. Nationally, more than half of this group rents, and many are divorced. This group tends to look for spiritual growth opportunities, along with help adjusting to divorce. The new multi-congregation youth ministry that Holy Trinity supports may be ministering with some families in this segment.

- "Established Country Families" are located in the direction of Hartfield. This segment is quite mixed economically and educationally. They are concerned about children, parenting, and schools, and tend to be looking for spiritual teaching. The new youth ministry may also touch the concerns of these families.

Holy Trinity selected a ten-mile radius as its study area. I would generally suggest that you create what Percept calls a custom polygon—an area

Figure 10: Worksheet for Studying Ministry Area Profile

Analysis of Major Population Groups

Name of group	% of pop	Characteristics	Est % of cong	Likely life concerns	Likely program preferences	Church strengths which might appeal to this group	What we might add or change to reach this group

bounded by a tailor-made combination of roads, rivers, town lines, or other features of your community—rather than using zip codes or automatically assuming that your ministry area fits exactly into your municipal boundaries. A custom polygon presses you to examine your assumptions more closely about the actual area in which you minister.

Discernment

As I have already mentioned, discernment is more of an attitude than a procedure. Powerful ministry emerges from a powerful connection with the holy. Prayer, song, silence, Scripture, creeds, confessions, saints, symbols, liturgies, histories—integrating these practices into your planning helps to root your explorations in sacred soil. They become channels of spiritual power for renewal. The suggestions offered in *Discerning Your Congregation's Future* are rich and varied. Another helpful writer on the subject of discernment is Charles Olsen (See *Transforming Church Boards* and *Discerning God's Will Together*.)[11]

Renewed Identity and Purpose

Though the "map" in figure 8 looks somewhat linear, this is not a mechanical process. Grappling with the content of each box in turn may provide shape to your explorations and help leaders work together more smoothly. But the process actually feels more like Jesus' parable of the mysterious reign of God, which emerges "as if someone would scatter seed on the ground, and would sleep and rise night and day, and the seed would sprout and grow, he does not know how" (Mark 4:26-17). Take a moment to record your initial thoughts generated by this chapter.

Renewed Identity and Purpose

1. What is our enduring faith-task, and what fresh form could it take today?

2. What do we wish to be known for in our community?

3. To what size are we called to aspire now?

4. What is the quality of life we seek within the congregations?

5. What guiding story or image crystallizes our vocation?

CHAPTER 4

Assessing Your Options

Unless a congregation reconnects faith with context in a fresh and powerful way, no strategy, structure, or program will make much difference in its long-term viability. Since the social context of the 1950s (or whichever decade was your "golden age") will never return, discernment of a renewed faith identity and purpose is essential.

A Spectrum of Choices

All of the following choices could be described by the general term "redefinition"—that is, a marked shift in the congregation's view of its own identity and purpose.

- Relocation to a new site.
- Merger with one or more surrounding congregations.
- Dramatic transformation involving one or more of the following:
  a) The congregation makes a significant change in the style or schedule of its worship to reach a broader population.
  b) The congregation moves from one size category to another, often from "family" (attendance 0 to 50) to "pastoral" (51 to 150) or "program" (151 to 350). Changing size requires a major shift in the congregation's culture.
  c) The make-up of both membership and leadership circles shifts markedly in economic level, race, ethnicity, language, culture, sexual orientation, age, or place of residence.
  d) The congregation adopts a significantly different model of ministry and leadership, one that does not involve a resident, seminary-trained

pastor. Sometimes characterized as "total ministry," this option applies particularly to congregations in isolated communities.[1]

- Parallel development (launching a new worshipping congregation on your site while maintaining a separate chaplaincy to the existing members in their familiar style).

If—after extended, prayerful exploration with outside help—all these options seem to suggest too much change, then you may not be experiencing a call to redevelopment ministry. In that case, other options might be:

- Part-time clergy (relieved of any expectation that they are going to "make the church grow").
- Yoked or cluster ministry (sharing clergy with other congregations to continue a modest but sustainable ministry on your current site).
- Hospice (planning a holy death that will richly honor the past—and perhaps bestow a legacy on another ministry that can carry forward your congregation's central faith values).

Some of these choices may be hard to consider right now, but it helps to keep a variety of options on the list and to keep exploring how each could be done well.

---

1. Which of these options has your church considered so far?

2. Which have been ruled out? Why?

3. What support might your congregation need in order to make a careful study of all the options before making a choice?

Relocation to a New Site

Some churches choose to launch a substantially new congregation by selling their existing site—often to an independent church that needs the space. Church consultant Lyle Schaller[2] estimates that you would need to purchase a "seven-to-twenty-acre site at a strategic location" to "make a fresh start for ministry in the twenty-first century." In this scenario, you would want to look for a pastor who has been selected and trained by your denomination to plant new churches. Most clergy are not trained to start something new from scratch. (See chapter 5 for suggestions about finding clergy leadership.)

Varying this theme a bit, you could become a two-site church:[3]

> Purchase the property for a second meeting-place. [Hold] an early service over there and the late service at your present site. Your new associate minister will follow a reverse schedule. This will require few changes for today's members but will open the door for new people to pioneer a new ministry at a new location.

Clearly, this approach requires enough capital to pay for land, a building, and the first year or two of a second clergy salary.

First Trinity Lutheran Church (Missouri Synod) employed both these strategies. Originally located in a downtown Buffalo, New York, site, this congregation purchased land in the early 1950s and opened a second location in an emerging suburban area—a move it was able to make because leaders faced facts early on. By about 1958, First Trinity moved away from the Buffalo site and consolidated its life at the new location in Tonawanda. In a recent envisioning process, members identified the possibility that they could launch a second site once again, in an area of newer suburban development.

What are the implications of a move? Relocation creates many of the same benefits as starting a congregation from scratch. First and foremost, there is a fresh encounter with context—an influx of new information, energy, and people made possible by the dissolution (or loosening) of the congregation's relationship with its previous setting. Since site and building shape a congregation's life so powerfully, moving to a new home will in itself reframe the church's identity to a significant extent. As a corollary to this first benefit, new potential emerges to reach a different generation. For example, younger baby boomers (born between 1956 and 1968) are "showing up in disproportionately large numbers in relatively new (or recently relocated), large, and rapidly-growing churches that offer a seven-day-a-week program."[4]

A congregation's attitude about relocating will probably reflect its theology and its institutional patterns. Sociologist Gerald Gamm has recently studied the historical trajectory of two religious groups—Jews and Roman Catholics—in the adjoining Boston neighborhoods of Dorchester and Roxbury. Because of segregated housing patterns in the region, the Great Migration of African-Americans into the Boston area from the early 1950s onward became heavily concentrated in Dorchester and Roxbury—communities dense with Jewish and Roman Catholic schools and congregations. In a time of rapid neighborhood change, these two religious traditions demonstrated markedly different understandings of the relationship between faith and context: Synagogues tended to relocate in the suburbs, while Roman Catholic parishes struggled to redefine their ministry in relation to neighborhood change. Carl Dudley and Sally Johnson's observations about the way congregational stories shape ministry seem relevant here—Jewish congregations may have mobilized energy for adaptation around "journey stories," as opposed to the "rooted stories" of Roman Catholic parishes. But Gamm also examines the dimension of "institutional rules."[5] He points first to the high degree of congregational autonomy within Judaism: "Responsible for their own survival, synagogues either moved or collapsed." In contrast, he notes that the institutional rules binding Roman Catholic parishes did not allow them to pull up stakes and follow their members to the suburbs; hence, these churches responded to a changing context by "reinforc[ing] residents' neighborhood attachments." Some expressions of "neighborhood attachment" were hostile to the newcomer. Nevertheless, the rooted character of Roman Catholic institutions gradually generated a commitment by the hierarchy to "maintain the spiritual and financial viability of inner-city parishes."[6] Able pastors initiated serious work on racial attitudes and community needs.

While a significant Roman Catholic institutional presence has continued into the 1990s, ministry is shifting again—this time toward community organizing. The Rev. John L. Doyle of St. Peter's Parish told Gamm:[7]

This parish is not viable right now. It is just a series of services. It runs a school, a dormitory, a women's shelter. But none of this is led by people in the parish. We have the shell, but the congregation is passive. Our instrument for making a difference is broad-based community organization. That is how Catholics can affirm their faith.

In response to Doyle's critique, Gamm observes that "the Catholic parish—with its monumental, outdated structures—is at least still present in these neighborhoods, and its presence is a necessary precondition for Doyle's work." (Two of the other urban congregations I will discuss in this section are significantly involved in broad-based community organizations like the one in Boston, drawing on methods of Chicago's Industrial Areas Foundation.)

What you decide about relocation has an important theological dimension. Especially in the "faith stories" of Episcopal and Lutheran churches, the concept of a geographical parish may still have a vital place—not merely as a throwback to days of legally established religion, but as a theological affirmation.[8] Since problems once labeled "urban" now manifest themselves in more and more communities, all congregations can draw important lessons from mainline churches that stay put and get down to work, connecting faith creatively to a tough context. Sometimes these churches can become vibrant centers for healing the urban-suburban split—as in the case of St. Gabriel's, Philadelphia, which we will examine later in this chapter.

1. Has your congregation ever talked about relocating? What were the pros and cons identified in that discussion? Why did or didn't the relocation occur?

2. Does your congregation have a "journey story" that might make relocation seem congruent with your faith identity? If so, where might that journey take you next?

3. Does your congregation have a "rooted story"—a sense of sacramental connection to its particular environment? If so, how could you become more deeply familiar with, and involved in, the lives of your neighbors and the major struggles of your community?

Merger with One or More Surrounding Congregations

Merger is a difficult category to discuss, because it is applied to several different strategies. I will try to tease them apart.

Combining two or more struggling churches on one of the existing sites. For the congregation whose building gets sold, this option is not usually very different from closing—except that it seems like bad manners to hold a proper funeral when we are supposed to be celebrating something new. If the members relinquishing their familiar site find the merger approach comforting, then it is certainly a reasonable choice. But everyone needs to understand that the resulting congregation will probably end up with no more members than the largest congregation going into the plan.

Why doesn't the consolidation of several weak congregations produce one strong one? Partly because it encourages people to focus inward. Often, merged congregations spend a lot of time deciding whose candlesticks will be used at Christmas and not much energy asking: "Who lives in this community today, and how could we reach them?" (The inability to answer that question creatively is part of the reason membership is declining in the first place.) Even if members decide to take a new look at identity and purpose, the work becomes tougher, since two or more narratives are involved.

Having tried my best to discourage you from seeing merger as a redevelopment strategy, I will tell an encouraging story. Brockton, Massachusetts, is a former manufacturing community south of Boston, known to most people in this metropolitan area through crime stories on the five o'clock news—a somewhat skewed representation of its life. Three Lutheran (ELCA) congregations in that vicinity pursued merger discussions over a period of years. One church, Christ the King, had a relatively new building in the neighboring town of Stoughton. One church, Gethsemane, was located in an old frame building on a main street of Brockton. The third church, Hope, was located in nearby Braintree.

At a certain point, when their discussions bogged down, they sought third-party help. In the first round of work, leaders of Gethsemane and Christ the King were interviewed separately, so that the sticky issues could be clarified. (Hope Church had decided to wait and re-enter the conversation later; they eventually joined into the plan.) It seemed as though both groups truly longed for unity, with each other and with Hope. But Christ the

King, which by now had sold its building and begun worshipping at Gethsemane, had two primary concerns. First, would something new actually be created, or would they just be folded into the style and habits of the larger congregation? Second (and equally important), would Gethsemane be willing to take a hard look at its own future viability? Leaders from Christ the King wanted to see the legacy they brought (proceeds from the sale of their property) really make a difference in generating new ministry. They didn't want the merger to become an excuse for the combined congregation to continue in slow decline.

Leaders of these two churches finally developed enough trust to take the leap, based on a set of agreements. As a unified congregation, members would choose a new name, develop a new charter, share leadership more equitably than numbers alone would dictate, establish a new worship schedule and format, renovate or rebuild the facility, and designate assets from Christ the King for a developmental purpose rather than for operations. And they agreed to do something that rarely works well—they called Christ the King's current pastor to lead the new congregation. Usually, retaining one or more of the current pastors impedes a fresh start, no matter what the clergy and congregation may intend. I don't recommend that you try it.

But the Rev. Beatrice Michals-Brown is a very unusual pastor. Trained in elementary education, she could not find any openings in that field when she started out at age 22. So she accepted a job teaching high-school students only five years her junior. "I had to get a group of 28 teenage boys to sit down and shut up," she says. "I knew every name and remembered something about each one personally. I looked like I expected them to do something. I was very organized, with a master plan; something specific was going to happen each day, and they were in for the ride."

At first glance, you might not pick out Pastor Beatrice as a likely candidate for the "entrepreneurial leader." You would be apt to mistake her for the elementary teacher she set out to be—steady, reassuring, unhurried, patient, and genuinely interested in listening to the people around her. But if you watch her interact with the congregation, you can see that this is a woman with a clear sense of purpose. The word that leaps to mind is "deliberate."

On a recent Sunday, I visited Prince of Peace. That's the new name of this "unified" congregation—members don't used the word "merger." As I parked across the street, I noticed a well-tended patch of lawn surrounding a large wooden cross (a symbol of Gethsemane's past identity)

- "Presents good ideas, but doesn't get upset if they aren't adopted."
- "Isn't afraid to ask people to do things; she gets some people we never thought of."
- "Has a nice way of doing things; she seems to get along."

These descriptions were a little confusing. Some people saw only the receptive side of Beatrice's style; others could identify the initiative side that helped moved things forward.

At the meeting itself I could see both sides of what they were describing. Beatrice set a calm, positive tone and asked group members how they thought leaders should be identified who might attend the training. Someone suggested phoning around. That idea provoked anxiety that people who weren't identified might feel left out. The "unity" theme surfaced: "If we want cohesiveness, we'd better be inclusive; people talk to each other." At one point, Beatrice asked directly for the thoughts of someone who hadn't been contributing; at another point, she summarized the idea that seemed to be gaining momentum.

After a period of discussion, Beatrice posed the problem again: "But how will we get people out to this meeting?" Discussion proceeded again, this time focusing on how big a turnout they actually needed or expected. Again she asked: "So how are we going to do it?" The group began examining the phone list. Someone suggested a notice in the newsletter; another member suggested a special letter. That idea provoked discussion about paying for mailings. After some more discussion, Beatrice did a reality check: "If we only send people a letter, do you think they'll really come?" A plan emerged that included several ways to contact people. Beatrice then "closed the deal" by summarizing what she had agreed to do, what she would ask the parish secretary to do, and what other members' jobs would be.

People call Beatrice a "good administrator," and her behavior in this meeting is part of what they are naming. She keeps the decision-making process moving along, makes sure all members are heard, focuses the group's attention on the central problem to be solved, challenges (with a question) solutions that sound unrealistic, and summarizes what has been decided. Members say that she keeps good records, reminds the group to check in with each other on tasks previously assigned, and helps the congregation maintain a healthy tension between support and accountability. Though selective about her interventions, she is also an initiator of new ideas for leaders to think about. Their growing interest in BIC is a seed she planted.

One final element puzzled me when I visited this church. From my television images of Brockton, I wondered how she, her husband, and their young child got the support they needed to live in a "tough" environment. Her answer was important: "Brockton is actually a good place to live. The press we get doesn't show a realistic picture. Brockton schools are good. We don't have an alarm system. And anyway, I'm from New Orleans!" Beatrice and her family are well-matched to this social context.

Closing existing congregations and combining resources for a new start. This approach requires that you secure a new, strategically chosen location; a new pastor; a new name; a new (or new-to-you) building; and a lot of new learning about what makes for church vitality. Most congregations thinking about merger cannot overcome the inertia of their current practices the way people did in Brockton. (That factor almost scuttled the Brockton plan before it started.) Very few have in place a pastor as well-suited to this work as Beatrice Michals-Brown—combined with a timely clergy vacancy in each of the other congregations. So if your goal is redevelopment (and not just a holding action) today's best advice about "merger" is: "Don't merge. Close the existing churches and start over somewhere else with some of the same people and some of the financial resources."

Only "some" of the existing people? Probably. For one thing, you already have members who would like to leave, but who don't want to betray their loyalty to a church they have loved. For another, the whole point of shaping a new identity is to reach people somewhat different from those who already attend; if it reaches others, that identity probably won't appeal to some of your current members. Perhaps most powerful of all, location matters. (Remember the old bromide about the top three factors for choosing a piece of real estate?—"Location, location, location.")

1. Has your congregation ever talked about merger? What were the pros and cons? Why did or didn't the merger occur?

2. Instead of merger, think about the option of closing several churches and making a combined new start on a different site. Do you think that this idea might generate interest, either in your church or in one or more neighboring congregations? How might this idea be interpreted and explored?

3. What hopes, values, and dreams of your congregation might become possible to realize, if only you could combine resources and start over?

Dramatic Transformation

Renowned church consultant Lyle Schaller gives the following advice to a pastor worried about serious numerical decline: "Instead of focusing on attracting new people, ask how much change this congregation will support, how much change it will tolerate, and what level of change will arouse immobilizing opposition."[9] I wish I had heard and absorbed this advice much earlier in my ministry. Like many clergy, I often overestimated the amount and pace of change I could initiate.

This advice doesn't mean, however, that congregations cannot undertake significant transformation. Sometimes a pastor can build support for an orderly and open process that will allow leaders to set a new direction for a congregation. Such an approach might include:

- *Assertive leadership by the pastor focused on enabling the process rather than on determining the final outcome*—using management and facilitation skills like the ones Beatrice Michals-Brown employed in Brockton.
- *Movement back and forth between broad participation and more focused strategic thinking by a smaller group.* In order to insure wide participation in the identification of options, Schaller suggests a

large "futures committee" appointed by the governing board—where church culture permits, two-thirds of the members might be nominated by the pastor. (Schaller's articles in *Net Results* can help such a group to develop their skills for generating many different scenarios before making judgments about them—an activity that few church committees have experienced).[10] In order to gain strategic focus, he recommends that a smaller team, including the pastor, draft a list of possible criteria for making the choice. One of these criteria should be the amount of change people will support.

- *Narrowing the list based on shared criteria.* Once a wide list of options has been developed, the possible criteria drafted for making the choice, the larger "futures committee" would have the job of "revising and ranking the criteria, and reduc[ing] the list to two scenarios," neither of which is the status quo.

- *Making a final decision between the two new approaches.* This choice would be made by the governing board or by congregational vote, depending on church polity. If a congregational vote is involved, Schaller recommends that several months be spent informing the membership about the choices.

- *Distinguishing the policy decision ("Which strategy will we follow?") from the implementation work.* Once a decision is made about the basic direction, it is wise for the board to appoint a new group to develop and monitor the action plan. In nominating people for this *ad hoc* team, focus on the gifts required for the new ministry—including passion for the basic goals and a variety of talents relevant to the work. Seek out the best leaders rather than waiting to see who volunteers.

Such a procedure works best when a congregation still has significant resources—people, energy, funds—that can be redirected into new ministry approaches. However, First Universalist Church in Woonsocket, Rhode Island, undertook a similar process when it was down to only 12 or 15 people at Sunday worship. The change they were willing to support was a new style of worship.

Transformation in Worship

Woonsocket was an early and innovative "mill city." First Universalist members exercised roles of civic and economic leadership, and ministers were known for their civic involvement—including a significant place in the development of public education and of an independent family-services agency. But by the end of World War II, Woonsocket and its churches were headed for decline. The city was bypassed by the emerging highway system and by the region's overall economic development.

In the 1950s, First Universalist still had an average attendance between 150 and 200 at a worship service that would have felt very comfortable to a Congregational or American Baptist visitor. The church had recently moved from its old prominent location on Main Street to a large lot in an adjoining residential neighborhood. It had built a capacious building and put in plenty of parking (though members say that the boxy shape of their edifice "doesn't look like a church" on the outside). In the early 1960s, the church joined the newly merged Unitarian-Universalist denomination, while still identifying themselves as a Christian body. In the 1960s adult attendance ran around 125 each week. By 1970, this number had dropped to 85, and by 1985 it was down to 30. The congregation remembers a "mass exodus" when a minister was asked to leave. The congregation split in two, and "the young people left." Though a number of major factors contributed to this trauma, one issue had to do with Christian identity. The minister had taken out the cross.

I met with the current minister, Peter Hughes, his wife Lynn, and members of the church for about nine months during 1996 and 1997. Sometimes it was very hard going, because both the city and the congregation seemed mired in severe depression. (The city was just beginning to build a bit of momentum for downtown revitalization, focused on a wonderful old-fashioned theater building on Main Street, but renewal still seemed a long way off.) Members seemed almost physically paralyzed in the meeting space, and rarely rose to meet an incoming guest.

Over the months, we worked our way through the issues delineated in chapter 3 under the heading "Reconnecting Faith and Context" (figure 8). The parish's historic identity and current resources included:

- Long history of concern for children, working families, and education.
- Sound, spacious building.
- Theater group using the building regularly (the church has an entire upper floor dedicated to this use).
- Good current connections to the area family-services agency.
- Good current connections to the local historical society.

- Modest endowment ($225,000).
- Willingness to try something new.

Opportunities identified in the external environment included:

- Possibility of cosponsoring a summer theater program for children with the theater company, and creating some sort of bridge with Sunday morning to bring people back.
- Possibility of an afternoon literacy program two days a week. One member was a literacy volunteer at the library, and the library was out of space.
- Many parents in the city were struggling to earn a living. The church might be able to help connect them with job opportunities now emerging in the Woonsocket area.

But as the group worked to create some possible scenarios, energy dropped. Any plan seemed doomed by two crucial weaknesses of the congregation:

- Once prospective members attended worship, they tended not to return. Twelve or 15 people were spread out in a space for 200; children and a few adults were off downstairs; the formal style (which had worked pretty well as long as the church was at least half full) seemed depressing with so few voices.
- The attempt to "keep everybody happy" was preventing anything new from happening. The board became paralyzed when anyone didn't like an idea.

At the point when it seemed that nothing would fly, Lynn Hughes proposed an idea—that the congregation work on integrating arts and creativity into the worship itself. This combination would serve the purpose of nourishing those who were already attending and would also create fresh energy which visitors might feel and respond to.

Who would lead such a ministry? Peter is highly knowledgeable about classical music, but he did not feel he had the right talents to design the kind of creative worship Lynn was describing. Shortly after this meeting, they heard about Monica-Lisa Mills, a laywoman with a divinity degree who was serving as chaplain at Rhode Island School of Design. Things moved quickly after that. The congregation voted to employ Monica part-time to make connections with the growing arts community in Woonsocket, and to share with Peter in the design and leadership of worship.

I visited the congregation in preparation for writing this book, and it was a wonderful experience. They had altered their tradition of summers "off" and scheduled a few Sunday services in July and August to maintain the continuity of their experimental worship offerings. As I approached the building through the parking lot, I noticed that a huge mural had appeared on a wall facing the church; a banner had been added to the blank side of the building facing the street; and a sign had been installed at the parish house door—"Center for the Arts and Spirituality." (I soon discovered that this "center" is a nonprofit organization established by the congregation as an outreach ministry into the Woonsocket community.)

About a dozen people had assembled by the appointed hour. The worship service took place in what had been an old-fashioned-looking parlor—now transformed into a bright, contemporary art-gallery space with good lighting. Quiet, chantlike music was playing from a CD boom box. Tables had been moved aside to create a circle of chairs just the right size for the group assembled. Monica, who presided at this service, is a slender, Mexican-American woman in her early 30s, combining a peaceful, loving presence with an artist's spontaneity and flair. The worship had the feeling of a dance, even though we were seated.

She lit the flaming chalice (a central symbol for Unitarian-Universalist worship) and invited those present to light a candle of their own for a special intention. She led the group in several quiet songs, including the summer verse of the haunting "Chant for the Seasons":[11]

> Gliding are the hawks, hovering above the hot and yellow hillside.
> Vernal clouds have turned the star-wheel, summer is upon us.

Monica read a passage from essayist-naturalist Annie Dillard about a hawk. The reading became a meditation on life and death. She then led the group gently in sharing and prayer. Many of us spoke about death and loss, but there was nothing depressing about the experience—a moment of wonder, mystery, and companionship had emerged out of simple elements.

As I spoke with the group over refreshments, it was clear that the church has had, and will have, big challenges to face. There is no guarantee that the new reality will take hold before the money runs out. But what a different conversation it was! Here is a little of that conversation:

SANDY [board chair]. It's exciting—not without problems, but a real positive thing. I have pride in the church; others see it in a good light. We're a cutting-edge religious organization, offering something for the community. Advise other churches to do what feels right despite the fear. You'll always be afraid. If you don't try, you'll never know. And we're having all this good experience trying!

LYNN. It's important not to lose faith in the process. We were exuberant at the beginning, but then the dailiness of it set in. Results are subtle, and take time to develop. You can't lose faith in the process just at the point when it's about to break through.

PETER. Monica posed a challenge—what can we do instead of the normal sermon-type service, to appeal to all the dimensions of the human being? It's both easier and harder; each week we have to ask, "What are we going to do?" Like jazz, it's not organized the same way—no score, but a plan. You don't know exactly how it will play out.

LLOYD. The program is successful—we should turn up the heat on the things that work, like the May Fair. We had a maypole and dancing, Canadian fiddle, workshops, raffles, a meal. All ages.

MARGARET. I didn't think we'd feed that multitude. Over 200 people came. The food was donated from local places.

PETER. Monica did a lot of the work and modeled how it could be done— now the congregation needs to pick up on responsibility. The center has a steering committee—almost all nonmembers from the local community. They did a lot of the work. Monica made relationships with the local businesses—she's good at nurturing relationships.

SANDY. Nobody comes without her talking to them about what's going on. She makes contact, people feel welcome, they want to come back. Now I try to do that, too.

MONICA. I come in on Monday and say, "Who was that person?"

SANDY [laughing]. Yeah, she's a pain in the butt!

MARGARET. Monica had a coffee house, with rock music. I love it.

LLOYD. We needed someone with a lot of natural enthusiasm. Chutzpah!

At this point in the conversation, Monica grew uneasy and spoke up:

> "Monica had a coffee house," "Monica had a concert"—when people say "we," I will have accomplished my job. My early months were frustrating. Meetings were pleasant, joking—but no one was

saying what was going on. When it seemed like there were underground complaints, I held back—I didn't want to be a troublemaker. But then came the moment when someone spoke about me as if I weren't there: "She. . . ." I turned around and said: "Who is she? I'm so tired of trying to make you happy!" I started crying and ran out. No one was at a place to emotionally handle what I had done. They just kept talking. I was outside in the lot sobbing; people went by me to their cars without saying anything.

This early crisis in Monica's tenure had exposed an "unwritten rule" of the congregation: "Go along with the leader during formal discussion, then complain to others about the results." In the two years that had elapsed between that painful confrontation and my recent visit, members of the leadership group had never discussed the incident all together. But individual leaders had drawn some immediate learnings from the crisis which led to new behavior. Monica adopted a new stance: "If you have something to say, say it! If not, I'm going ahead!" Sandy made an inner resolution: "I've been frustrated for years. This made me determined to say to board members, 'If you have a problem, if you want to know where that vase went, then I think you should inquire and report back to the next meeting.' Nobody has!" Lynn summarized the overall learning church leaders took away from the crisis: "If the goal is to avoid a scene, we can't avoid it by not responding; the scene will happen anyway."

Attendance at First Universalist has approximately doubled since 1996—the congregation now has 25 to 35 people at Sunday morning worship (including children). The church is drawing more first-time visitors and seeing more people come back on a regular or occasional basis. Currently, the worship is "blended"—alternating between more traditional and more contemporary styles on different weeks. To accelerate membership growth, a second service may be started on Sunday evenings, always in the more innovative style and regularly led by Monica. (This approach would create a situation resembling "parallel development," described later in this chapter.) Since Peter is retiring this summer, leaders are in the process of choosing an interim minister. Recognizing the need for grant-writing and fund-raising around their emerging identity, they will seek a candidate who can assist with these tasks. The congregation has recently learned that the denomination makes three-year grants for "extension ministry"; while First Universalist has to gain more members before it can qualify, this program offers some concrete targets and greater hope for viability. A new service, an interim minister with fund-raising skills, and an extension-ministry grant from the denomination might combine to put this church back on the road to financial viability. All that may still not be enough. But the members are having a wonderful time trying.

This example reveals both the importance and the difficulty of transforming worship to reconnect a congregation with its context. It has taken two years for the church to gain some confidence about its newer worship style. Members have felt a need to alternate traditional and innovative services. Monica Mills still experiences some resistance on Sunday morning if she goes "too far" outside the experience of some long-term members in her creative worship experiences.

The recent work of church-growth specialist Charles Arn[12] has persuaded me that redevelopment congregations should seriously consider adding a new worship service rather than trying to blend the old and the new—particularly when institutional resources are too low for a long incremental process. Many of the assumptions that discourage church leaders from trying a new service were found by Arn to be invalid. For example, it is not true that small churches can't add worship opportunities—a church with an attendance of 40 or more is big enough to start a second service. Nor it is true that only growing churches should add a worship service; indeed, decline is an even stronger signal to try something new.

Further, leaders often assume that they should start an additional service only when the sanctuary is full.[13] Arn found some interesting, counterintuitive relationships between seating capacity and the success of a new worship opportunity. When the church is less than 40 percent full, a new service is *especially* appropriate because the current service is unlikely to grow, and its attendance is unlikely to be diminished by the new service. Adding a service is touchier matter in a church whose attendance has remained plateaued for several years at 60 to 80 percent of seating capacity, because the new service under those conditions may well draw off some of the current service's strength. Even so, says Arn, starting a new worship opportunity still creates the greatest likelihood of an overall increase in attendance. In the case where a church is actually filled up already (80 to 100 percent of capacity), he recommends the immediate creation of an *identical* service, rather than one of a somewhat different style.

Arn has identified several strong reasons for expanding the worship opportunities and the range of worship styles. First on the list is the effect on those who are not worshipping anywhere. Planning for a new service helps a congregation focus its attention on those who are not here yet, challenges leaders to convey the core message in fresh ways, and makes it easier for people to invite friends and neighbors. This last point is worth emphasizing. People often hesitate to invite because they don't have confidence that their church's familiar patterns will "connect" with others; when a meaningful new opportunity is planned, the number of invitations increases dramatically.

The increased variety of times and styles will also minister better to the range of people who are already on your church rolls active and inactive. The broader culture today fosters in people the expectation that they will have choices in their religious involvements, right along with other aspects of their lives. Offering another major worship opportunity at a different time, and in a somewhat different style, guarantees that more kinds of people can participate in our church life without disrupting the patterns that have proved meaningful for many current members. A blended approach (older and newer elements in the same service) often ends up frustrating everyone, and undermining the financial stability of the congregation in the process.

---

1. If your congregation were to transform its worship to connect better with people in your context today, what might that new worship look like?

2. Has your congregation ever had more than one worship service? If so, what differing needs were filled by the two services (even if they were rather similar in style)?

3. If you do not currently have more than one weekend worship opportunity, what advantages do you see to this approach?

Size Change as Dramatic Transformation

Many congregations seeking redevelopment have slipped down into "family size," both in numbers (average attendance below 50) and in dynamics (a small, intimate circle of members governed by a few matriarch-patriarch figures.) Though such a church may experience initial success in its evangelism efforts, it will probably bump into the "glass ceiling" of a size plateau when it hits the zone between 50 and 70 in average attendance. Unless the congregation undertakes a dramatic transformation in its self-concept, its "way of being church," it will not continue to grow past the plateau zone. (Other plateau zones exist at attendance levels of 150 to 200, and 350 to 400.) Hence, it is important for congregations attempting redevelopment to understand the dynamics of size transition.

At the threshold between one size category and another, the potential for incremental growth and change runs out, and a whole new form is required if the church is to move fully into the next size. Here is my own brief description of the four church sizes first identified by church sociologist Arlin Rothauge.[14]

The family size church (0 to 50 attending) is a single-cell organism—a social system resembling an extended biological family in which "we all know each other." As in actual families, some members are added by birth or marriage, while others are incorporated rather slowly and carefully in a process of adoption. Given the small membership numbers in such churches, clergy are usually part-time and short-term. Though they are permitted to function as chaplains to the family, the leadership that actually holds these churches together comes from the matriarchs and patriarchs—anchoring figures who maintain stability through their tacit authority. A healthy family-size church is usually known in its community for one vibrant ministry focus, often some form of direct service to the community offered in a "down-home" style.

The pastoral size church (50 to 150) is a multicell organism—a coalition of several overlapping family-friendship networks unified around the person and role of the pastor. When a congregation is portrayed in literature, in films, or on television, it is often made in this "pastoral" image: a church on the green with its resident parson. At its best, this congregation is big enough to look to the visitor like a "real church," and small enough to feel personal. If the pastor is suited to the community and has a good team relationship with the board, harmony and spiritual coherence can result.

However, churches with attendances under 100 cannot usually support a full-time clergy position, and may experience frequent pastoral turnover. A healthy pastoral-size church is usually known in its community for two or three strong ministries, including worship with a personal touch.

The program size church (150 to 350) is known, as the name suggests, for the quality and variety of its programs. Its larger and more diverse membership will contain a "critical mass" of people from several different age and interest groups—children, youth, couples, seniors, etc. This substantial presence of varied populations stimulates creative ministry and provides entry points for new members from different demographic groups. Typically, part- and full-time staff are added as programs are initiated or strengthened, but the ministries of members also expand into such areas as pastoral care, new-member incorporation, community outreach, and the leadership of small groups for sharing and prayer about members' own life circumstances. At its best, the program church's excellent processes for democratic participation create a sense of excitement, purpose, and possibility.

The corporate size church (350 to 500-plus) is a significant institutional presence in its community. It may have a cathedral-like building in a prominent location, associated institutions like a day school or community center, and a sizable staff of highly skilled professionals. This larger congregation can provide "something for everybody"—a variety of different kinds of worship, education, spiritual nurture, and social interaction. It also provides a visitor the chance to remain anonymous for a while—a plus for some people in urban settings who may not want to make commitments right away. Sometimes this congregation attracts into membership key leaders from the wider community because of its substantial public presence. "Tall-steeple churches" usually seek "tall-steeple pastors"— clergy with a sufficient symbolic presence to focus a large worship service, head an extensive staff, and challenge powerful lay leaders with a bold and unifying purpose.

Between sizes, congregations that have been growing steadily tend to hit an attendance plateau. Once a church enters that threshold area, the strength and appeal of the previous size are already compromised, while the virtues of the next size are not in place. Leaders find themselves in a lose-lose position because two competing sets of expectations are laid upon them. Confusion, anxiety, and indecision often result—until the members honestly and deeply engage the choice before them. In a size transition, churches are especially susceptible to those two destructive illusions I have already identified—the fantasy of growth without change, and the fantasy of change without conflict. With study, prayer, and (often) some outside guidance, congregations can navigate successfully through size transitions. Appendix B contains a chapter from my book *The In-Between Church*, describing in more detail what happens in the movement between sizes.

1. Which of the four size descriptions sounds most like your congregation? Why?

2. What other sizes has your congregation been in the past? Are any "ghost structures" from those previous sizes still hanging around your church? (E.g., by-laws that specify a quorum bigger than your current congregation; or a worship space with plenty of seats for the ghosts of your 1950 membership.)

3. If your worship attendance grew by 30 percent, would it put you into a new size category? For this to occur, your congregation's self-image will probably have to shift to resemble the description for that new size category. How do you feel about such a shift?

Dramatic Racial and Cultural Transformation

Racial and cultural transformation has been one of the most difficult types of change for mainline churches to undertake—a painful truth for denominations like my own that often take progressive positions on social issues. We speak passionately about inclusiveness but remain remarkably homogeneous.

The multicultural faith community is still a "countercultural" project in American society. In other words, it challenges a host of social norms and institutional patterns. This observation pertains whether we are speaking of an individual congregation that brings different races and cultures together at one table, or of a multicultural denominational fellowship that nurtures and celebrates the development of many effective specialized ministries. Rich spiritual exchange across cultures is a radical aspiration.

St. Gabriel's Episcopal Church, Philadelphia, is a vibrant congregation where cultures meet. This was not the case in 1981, when I completed a brief period of service as this church's part-time pastor. At that time the church was barely emerging from decades of decline. I recall many Sundays with 10 to 20 worshippers, little cultural mix, and hardly any program beyond weekly worship. Today, the average Sunday attendance is 68—more than triple the numbers I remember—and the congregation swells to as many as 140 at major celebrations.

St. Gabriel's is located at the corner of Front Street and Roosevelt Boulevard—the oldest edge of residential expansion into the "Great Northeast," which began in the 1920s. The church's immediate neighborhood—Olney—and the adjoining neighborhoods of Feltonville and Logan once made up an appealing and comfortable community for families whose breadwinners worked in manufacturing, sales, clerical jobs or skilled trades. Major employers were the Sears-Roebuck catalog sales center and Heinz Foods. People came to this area to live in attractive, two-story, semi-detached homes, built of gray stone or red brick. The boulevard in the earlier days was quite obviously an extension of Fairmount Park, with broad, tree-lined median strips dividing the lanes, and park-guard booths at the major intersections. Three public secondary schools in Olney—Central, Girls', and Boys' high schools—were prestigious magnet institutions for academically talented students, many of whom went on to college at the University of Pennsylvania or Temple University.

These communities thrived during World War II, partly because of defense-related employment opportunities and good public transportation. But, like other city neighborhoods in the postwar period, they could not compete with the automobile suburbs for the more affluent and mobile segments of the white middle class. Because of federal housing policy, families could more easily obtain mortgages on newly constructed homes in the city's "far northeast" and its adjoining suburbs than for the purchase of homes in established neighborhoods. Racist practices in real estate funneled African-American families seeking homes into one urban neighborhood at a time, exacerbating racial tensions. Riots in nearby North Philadelphia in the late 1960s hastened the exodus of white families who had the resources to move out.

Although a significant degree of "urban renewal" has recently occurred in Philadelphia's downtown district and a few upscale areas, the quality of life is eroding (at best) in most city neighborhoods. Near the church, for example, 956 homes started sinking into the ground 18 years ago; the city's sluggish response has left some residents and squatters still inhabiting a ghost town. Residents of the 55-acre area have been fighting for seven years for the cleanup of soil contamination caused by sewage, paint, and dumping; children play each day in back yards laced with lead, arsenic, and mercury. Drug houses abound in the vicinity of the church. Conditions like these in neighborhoods around the city cause 83 people a day to move out of Philadelphia.[15]

While such challenges might cause an outsider to write off the church's location as a complete liability, St. Gabriel's has discovered on this site springs of spiritual strength and rich opportunities for ministry. Forty-three languages are spoken in the community surrounding the church, and the congregation vibrates with similar cultural variety. Its membership includes people of African-American, West Indian, Puerto Rican, Costa Rican, Nigerian, Liberian, Chinese, Alaskan Native, and Haitian birth or descent (together composing about half the membership); seven or eight households I still remember from the early 1980s, reflecting the earlier identity of the neighborhood; and a substantial group of newer white members—some highly involved with community organizations, public education, and the arts.

St. Gabriel's pastor ("vicar" in Episcopal terminology) is the Rev. Mary Laney, a vital, outgoing, blond-haired woman who looks younger than her 58 years. Having grown up in Philadelphia neighborhoods not too far from St. Gabriel's, she devoted the first part of her adult life to raising a family with her husband, Earl. Through involvement with the Home and School Association (where she soon landed on the executive board) and other voluntary organizations, Mary developed a keen understanding of organizational politics. "I would observe how it works," she says, "at dancing school or Girl Scouts. I figured out who had power." She also developed an acute sense of responsibility for making things better, especially in the church. Both her parents had been deeply involved in their parish, which had turned into a very troubled situation by the time Mary had reached her teens. Coming out of this early experience with congregations, Mary says, she has developed an antenna to tell her when "something is wrong here."

As she approached 40, Mary began to think about ordination. First she had to go to college—graduating the same year as her oldest daughter—then to seminary in New York. When she returned to Philadelphia, hoping for an appointment to an urban congregation, the bishop's office urged her to get experience at a large, affluent suburban church, where she served as an assistant for several years. In 1989, Mary was appointed full-time vicar of St. Gabriel's—one of the financially aided congregations that form the Diocesan Coalition for Mission and Ministry—to replace the Rev. James Davis, a priest who had served for the previous four years and was now moving out of state.

Jim Davis—the first full-time priest at St. Gabriel's in many years—had helped the congregation to make its first tentative steps toward racial and cultural change. When a West Indian woman visited the church, Jim immediately followed up; as a result, she started to attend with her niece and two nephews. In a similar way, the first African-American household joined the church. With the help of two interns preparing for ordination, the church made an attempt to reach the area's Spanish-speaking population. "Even though there were only 20 or 22 people when I arrived," Mary says, "there were enough who were relatively new to the church. There was some cultural mix. They were beginning to identify themselves that way."

About the same time Mary arrived, the Rev. John Midwood became archdeacon—a position on the bishop's staff providing oversight for struggling congregations receiving diocesan financial assistance. When John arrived on the bishop's staff, he was troubled that many in the diocese grudgingly viewed the funding of urban ministry as "welfare." "Needs were growing," he says, "and it seemed there was always just enough funding to leave everybody frustrated"—even before the program encountered a funding crisis in 1990. During that year, some grants were cut back as clergy vacancies occurred. By the next year, a new system went into place, which reduced (over a period of time) the total number of churches receiving continuing financial assistance from the diocese.[16]

The emerging strategy for urban ministry centered on a group of congregations newly designated as "diocesan missions." The bishop's office invited these eight[17] churches into a closer partnership, aimed at fulfilling the diocese's overall mission in the cities. Pastors were referred to as "our urban missionaries," and the diocese assumed full responsibility for providing adequate clergy salary and benefits. The congregation was expected to do the hands-on ministry in its community and to generate funds for its own programs and facilities.

One major result of this policy has been stability in clergy leadership. "The system has worked so well that there is little turnover. We set the midpoint [of the diocesan salary scale] as our standard for the well-seasoned, experienced clergy who serve in these locations," says John Midwood.

Another result is focused ministry: The clergy give their full attention to their task of missionary leadership. John spends little of his time worrying about these eight missions because local leaders take full responsibility for developing good ministry together. Later in the book, I will discuss the controversial nature of this funding strategy. Here, this description simply provides part of the background for understanding how one astounding transformation occurred.

Mary's early days at St. Gabriel's involved "clearing out junk and learning who people were." She planned a series of Lenten home meetings to talk about Scripture and the symbolic meanings of the cross. She recalls how a key lay leader, George Clyde, "hauled me around to community groups and I said yes to everything," including involvement in the Olney Neighborhood Center and Olney Community Council. Mary's high level of availability to the community soon paid off. Members of the Olney Community Council requested use of the St. Gabriel's basement for an after-school program. Mary made it clear that the church could provide only space—others in the community would have to arrange for program leadership and funding—and the program began.

Even Mary, with her organizational savvy, never imagined what difficulties St. Gabriel's was about to face. Staffing issues and financial management turned out to be a nightmare. And despite the clear boundaries Mary had set on the congregation's involvement at the beginning of the partnership, the church's reputation in the community was soon on the line. "People thought it was [a] St. Gabriel's program; it looked like we had promised something we couldn't deliver. Our key commitment was to build trust with the neighborhood—if they can't believe us about this, why should they believe us about the Gospel?" First, the church collaborated with community leaders, devising a plan to keep the center open one day a week with volunteers. Then, when Mary was out of town on retreat, another crisis broke—all the volunteers quit after an argument with a church staff member. Mary left the retreat to deal with the situation, recognizing at that moment that she was fully committed to see this program succeed.

With the help of an intern from the diocesan school for deacons, St. Gabriel's generated a foundation grant underwriting the salary of a half-time director to run the program with a volunteer team. Within four to six months, this new job was expanded to a full-time position. The refocused program, now called "AAA Kids Program," used art as the "great leveler"—a medium that could bridge differences in language, culture, class, and educational background. "If we could build it with children, " Mary Laney said, "we could use that trust to create some relationships with parents, and with each other in the congregation."

Before long, parents started talking to the center's staff about the need for academic help. So the program developed a distinctive format that is still the nucleus of its work, involving 40 children at a time from grades one through eight. (More than 300 children have participated since 1990, and 100 are still on the waiting list.) The children have a half-hour of transitional activities to "get them there"; an hour of help with their homework; an hour in an arts activity (dance, music, painting); then another transitional half-hour of games. This pattern is supplemented by special trips, health screenings, an FBI safety program, Sierra Club presentations about the environment, and Fridays with a visiting artist.

An exciting relationship has developed over the past few years with staff at Olney Elementary School. In the midst of a children's mural project in the school building, Mary got to know the interim principal. He in turn introduced her to one of the school's nonteaching staff, Dwight James—an African-American man with a deep devotion to children, who is also a professional musician and a teacher of percussion instruments. Initially, he offered his musical talent to help children in the after-school program prepare a presentation for "parent's evening." But Mary said: "This is too good to stop now; people have to see these kids." When they started to book performances at city and suburban churches (and even at the Camden County Music Festival), it became apparent that the group needed a name. Dwight James suggested they use the Swahili word for "children," and the group thereafter became the Watotos. Thirteen students in grades five through eight now prepare for eight to ten performances a year. And the group has just released its first compact disc.

Since 1990, when the after-school program first opened, widening circles of ministry have emanated from St. Gabriel's: a literacy center, art residencies in neighborhood schools, "Olney OK Kids" for at-risk ninth graders, "Vacation Ventures" summer day camp, and a center for computer training. The church reaches a thousand children and adults each year in one or more of these programs. All of the programs are now incorporated under the banner of "Urban Bridges at St. Gabriel's." This nonprofit corporation with a $350,000 budget is guided by its own board—half from suburban congregations, half from the parish and the Olney community. Every member of the board has some kind of hands-on involvement with the program:

driving the Watotos to a concert, helping to host a parent night, even volunteering one day a week. The vicar either chairs the board or appoints the chair: "It's important," Mary says, "for St. Gabriel's to understand that this is their mission."

From the beginning, both John Midwood and Mary Laney put first priority on faith in the expansion of ministry at St. Gabriel's. "What makes it a church," says Midwood, "is the gathering of a religious community week by week; that's a unique dimension that can't be replicated by any other agency." Laney echoes this emphasis: "This work all depends on your openness to what God can do in your midst with what you have now—even with an apparent weakness like this location." The authenticity of the faith venture at St. Gabriel's is apparent in its worship.

Returning to St. Gabriel's on a recent summer Sunday was a profoundly hopeful experience. Like the rest of its neighborhood, the stone-and-slate church building from the late 1920s always had a modest charm. But the property has never looked as lively as it does today. A large sign on the lawn welcomes the community in five languages. The former rectory on the corner has been remodeled into offices, a computer lab, and a basement activity room. On the wall facing Front Street (and looking toward the sinking homes a little further south) is an enormous mosaic representation of an angel with words from Luke: "I am Gabriel. I stand in the presence of God, and I have been sent to speak to you and to bring you this good news. With God, all things are possible." On the front steps of the church, people were greeting each other with joy and warmth.

Their celebration of the Holy Eucharist would have felt familiar to most Episcopalians around the country—yet the experience was filled with spiritual energy generated by the encounter between the Gospel and these particular circumstances. I was immediately struck, for example, by the way people related to the prayer books and hymnals in their pews. With so many recent immigrants in this community and so much emphasis on literacy in the congregation's outreach, reading—whether of Scripture, prayers, or hymn texts—is a sacred activity in which everyone fully participates, right down to the smallest acolyte. Mary is conscious of providing every opportunity for this kind of participation.

The music was a mixture of older standard hymns ("Joyful, joyful, we adore thee"), new standards from the praise genre ("Seek ye first the kingdom of God"), and spirituals from the Lift Every Voice and Sing, a supplemental Episcopal hymnal ("Mine eyes have seen the glory" and "There's a sweet, sweet Spirit"). Several of the selections were accompanied by blues-style harmonica, and one piece was sung as a round with the help of two impromptu conductors. Everyone took part in the singing—even in the sung parts of the liturgy itself.

This particular Sunday marked the beginning of a new practice—occasional sermons by members of the congregation. Mary says, "I would hear people share things in Bible study or discussion and I would notice the wisdom and power in it. It's important that they don't see clergy as having the Scripture all locked up—that they are willing to share how God works in their lives." So at this service, the preacher was Lauriel Cabrall, a woman born in St. Kitts, who serves as vicar's warden (the chief lay officer of the congregation). She began by affirming both herself and the congregation: "The Holy Spirit is moving through St. Gabriel's, calling new people to new ministries." Reflecting on the day's scriptural reference to David, she addressed the congregation forthrightly: "Brothers and sisters at St. Gabriel's, you can become like David, a commander and a leader; you have no idea what you can become." The sermon ended with a further affirmation: "Jesus is saying to us, 'Nothing is impossible'"—a wonderful echo of Gabriel's declaration to the Virgin Mary, represented on the mosaic wall outside.

At the time for prayers, a book containing people's special concerns was brought forward and placed on the altar so that communion could be celebrated over it. Considerable time was provided for people to speak spontaneously about the blessings in their lives that week, and many had something heartfelt to share. One thanked God for a medical test with a hopeful result, another for one full year as a member of the church. A man in traditional African garb gave thanks for the shift from military to civilian rule in Nigeria, while another spoke of being pulled up "out of the deep dark water" of a painful family situation.

One distinctive ritual generated by the people themselves has been added to the weekly liturgy in this church. It started when someone asked to sing, "Let there be peace on earth." Then came the request, "Can't we do it every week?" People started to hold hands in the pew when they sang it. Then someone suggested they get out of the pews and make one big circle all around the church, which they now do weekly after everyone has received communion. In some settings, this ritual might seem a bit sentimental. Here it felt profoundly sacramental to look into all the faces— knowing tragic stories of addiction, domestic violence, exile from homeland, police brutality, lost children, life-threatening illness, depression, and all the rest—but at the same time seeing the wholeness of the circle and the sense of spiritual empowerment represented in the words "Let it begin with me." Mary is aware of the liturgical criticism that might be leveled at such a ritual, but she says that this ministry requires a "willingness to try something that you don't completely understand. There are no rules—other than connecting people with God in a healthy way."

The ministry at St. Gabriel's has two other dimensions that should be noted here. First, the congregation participates in the Philadelphia Interfaith Alliance—a community-organizing effort based on the same principles as the one in Brockton, Massachusetts. On the Sunday I was there, a member of the congregation announced that a few people would be attending a PIA training opportunity focusing on skills for building relationship in communities. A leaflet was available in church that day which detailed the plight of the people in the sinking homes. Written by a neighboring Baptist pastor who is active as a PIA leader, the handout told the story of one family in the pastor's own congregation—then related that story to city policies and priorities. Through its member congregations, PIA mobilizes community residents into an independent force with enough power to effect some changes in the city's quality of life.

Mary commented on the question of leadership development in communities like the one she serves. People who show potential may leave the neighborhood when they gain enough resources to move on; or they may "sink back into the darkness" of addiction and violence. For people who stay and try to make a difference in community organizations and public schools—like several members of St. Gabriel's and Mary herself—the danger is burnout and anger. She struggles with the challenge of helping people to be good stewards of their own energies, so that they can help maintain a stable presence.

And finally, I will note an aspect of the ministry at St. Gabriel's that would not have been apparent to me without some interpretation. Mary and other leaders give enormous attention to the spiritual growth of volunteers who participate in some way in the St. Gabriel's ministry. "One of our most important roles is to be a place where people from suburban congregations can explore and express their faith in concrete ways. Sometimes people want to treat us like stepchildren. When they come, they often leave in tears. Sometimes they get scared and don't come back." But many volunteers from suburban churches do stay involved with St. Gabriel's and find the experience transformative. Before she ever came to St. Gabriel's, Mary had been working energetically for many years to build partnerships between urban and suburban churches, and today this is a central theme in the way she understands her work. Without the opportunity for life-changing relationships that bridge the canyon between city and suburbs, she believes that her diocese would lose its soul.

1. To what extent is there a racial and cultural gap between your congregation (membership) and the community you serve?

2. How do you feel about that gap?

3. What help might be available to your church if you decided to explore the possibility of dramatic racial or cultural transformation?

Transformation in Model of Ministry and Leadership

In geographically isolated communities, redevelopment may mean something quite different from what I have described so far. Frequently in these settings, family-size and small pastoral-size churches struggle to secure even part-time clergy leadership. If they are able to find pastors, turnover may be high; or on the other end of the spectrum, they may feel "stuck" with a pastor who isn't a good match but is the only person available. On the other hand, pastors may not be as big a problem as lay leadership dynamics. The tacit authority of matriarchs and patriarchs—which can function as a loving anchor for many creative member ministries—can also stand as a barrier to the kind of adaptation I have been calling for throughout this book. The word "tacit" is the key: Congregations generally cannot change any dynamic that they cannot name, discuss, and negotiate, especially around issues of authority.

Whether your church is able to pay for a modest building and part-time staff, or whether you are draining your budget to meet salary guidelines for seminary-trained clergy, your congregation may feel locked into old patterns of authority and leadership based on unhealthy kinds of dependency. In that case, you might want to explore a pattern that is sometimes called "total ministry." This term has been employed for 20 years or more by Episcopal leaders in the western United States—especially in Nevada—and in many other parts of the world to describe an approach to congregational renewal focused on ministry development.

"Total ministry" is not a single model of parish organization. Rather, it is a way of looking at some radically different options for congregational life, beginning with the assumption that:

- Baptism, rather than ordination, provides the essential authorization for Christian ministry, both in the world and within the congregation.
- The congregation is a ministering community, rather than a community gathered around a "minister."
- Members can learn (with the help of wise guides from outside the congregation's "family circle") new ways of ministering to each other and to their surrounding community.
- Sacramental, pastoral, educational, and administrative ministries can be supplied by a team of four or five members, who are identified through a careful congregational discernment process.
- While extensive training and formation are essential for this ministry team, going away to seminary is not the only (or even the best) preparation for their role.

"Total ministry" sounds deceptively simple to some congregations. In a sense it is—in the same way that an admonition like "Love thy neighbor" is simple. In practice, the route to understanding and realizing this vision of communal ministry is likely to be long, bumpy, and spiritually demanding. (This is why I have included "total ministry" in the list of dramatic transformations.)

"Total ministry" also requires a good support system within your denominational structure. Where a local church does well with this team approach, it is usually part of a well-staffed middle-judicatory support network that might include:

- Strong and informed support from denominational leaders and departments.
- Local training schools designed especially for this new form of ministry.
- Seminary-trained clergy with special talents serving as "area ministers" or "regional vicars"—providing intensive support through the whole

developmental process (and beyond) for congregations learning how to do this kind of ministry.

Your denomination may already have some model in place that resembles the one I have described here. Or you might initiate an exploration with denominational staff in your region, starting perhaps with joint study of Stewart Zabriskie's book *Total Ministry: Reclaiming the Ministry of All God's People.*[18]

---

1. What, if any, aspects of "total ministry" seem relevant to the situation of your own congregation?

2. Who in your denominational structure might be able to discuss with you some similar models?

3. If you feel further study of this option would be helpful, who might join you in some reading and discussion about it?

Parallel Development

The final approach to redevelopment I will describe may actually overlap with some of the others on the list. Near the beginning of any redevelopment effort, a critical choice is made—whether to undertake a new era of ministry on one track or two. Most of the congregations I have worked with start out insisting that we all must stay together, and that new members must be brought into the existing circle. If you have plenty of time for incremental change, and if the people in your community today are not too different from you, this approach might work. Recall the story of First Universalist in Woonsocket. They have spent two years and a considerable amount of their remaining endowment to create an appealing Sunday-morning experience, well-linked with a "feeder" system to draw potential members (the high-profile arts ministry that brings the congregation into frequent contact with unchurched people in the community.) This is what I would characterize as a "one-track" redevelopment effort—we all change together, and we blend and balance the needs to find a style everyone can at least "live with."

If this church stays on one track, I believe that Sunday worship is likely to reach a plateau at an average attendance around 50. First Universalist's current approach tends to filter out potential members who have a strong preference either for the more traditional or for the more creative worship style, and it prevents each of those styles from evolving naturally along its own trajectory. Blending in worship involves a complicated political settlement which is fiendishly hard to renegotiate. This may well be the moment for First Universalist to switch to a "parallel development strategy"—two distinctive tracks of ministry, each with its own worship service.

Parallel development[19] makes significant demands on the congregation's leaders and members. When a single shared style is no longer the basis of unity, the congregation must articulate an underlying vocation big enough to encompass both tracks of development. New power arrangements must also be worked out—if the old guard tries to control the newer ministry, or if the innovators cast aside the old-timers, the congregation's climate will be inimical to both spiritual and numerical growth. Several foundational principles will typically undergird this power arrangement:

- The newer ministry—aimed at reaching the people who live around this church today—has a claim to "prime time." The ideal time slot for the new worship option may not be Sunday morning at all. But if it is, leaders make a commitment to adjust anything that may be necessary to give that new worship service its very best chance to succeed (Sunday morning time schedule, furniture arrangement, musical instruments, areas of the building utilized—anything).

- The chaplaincy ministry—worship and pastoral care with an emphasis on continuity for longer-term members—is guaranteed to continue as long as it is needed. Sometimes a more traditional worship option actually grows a bit numerically when attempts to blend (and the concomitant political tensions) are relinquished. Sometimes the old-timers discover that they want to refresh their own worship with some new twists—which they may now be free to undertake because no one is demanding that they change. The chaplaincy group may not, however, demand that others in the congregation worship with them; the style they evolve for themselves, with the support of the pastor, must be one which they can realistically implement at the size they actually are today.

- The redevelopment pastor agrees to support and care for both congregations. I would recommend that the pastor be expected to spend at least two-thirds of his or her time developing the church's newer "track"—since the congregation's future existence probably depends on the vitality of this new ministry.

Parallel development seems to be used frequently to develop Spanish-speaking ministries within the framework of existing Anglo- or African-American congregations.

---

1. What advantages might parallel development provide to your congregation's redevelopment effort?

2. What costs and difficulties would parallel development involve?

3. How long will your congregation exist if you do not make a strong new connection with your community? If your timeline is 15 years or less, do you think that parallel development might offer a better chance of success than incremental change?

CHAPTER 5

What Do We Do Next?

Perhaps you have come to believe that your congregation needs the kind of dramatic change signified by the term "redevelopment." If that is the case, then the worst thing you can do right now is to grab hold of an "answer"— from this book or from other research—and try to sell it to your members. No strategy, structure, or program will make much difference in the long-term viability of your church unless you go back to the fundamental question: *How will we connect our deepest faith-identity to the realities of our context today?* If I were to apply an academic metaphor, I would say: "This question requires an essay answer, not a multiple-choice checkoff."

Stay with the Questions

If you go back and review some of the moments when your congregation grappled with its choices about the future—perhaps in the course of selecting a pastor, allocating endowment funds, debating liturgical renewal, or responding to denominational initiatives—you may find that leaders and members demanded a clear, quick answer. We human beings tend to believe that somebody "out there" has the solution to our fundamental life questions. We greet potential answer-givers initially with hope and adulation (whether they are political candidates, medical researchers, or the latest management gurus), and then we demolish them with our rage when we discover that our life is not "fixed."

What our souls actually crave, deeper down, is human and divine companionship on this mysterious journey of our lives. Sandy, the board chair at First Universalist in Woonsocket, was speaking from a firsthand experience of such spiritual companionship when she said: "If you don't try, you'll never know. And we're having all this good experience trying!" One of my favorite hymns speaks of openness to the mystery of divine companionship in the idiom of 13th century Europe:[1]

Humbly I adore thee, Verity unseen,
who thy glory hidest 'neath these shadows mean;
lo, to thee surrendered, my whole heart is bowed,
tranced as it beholds thee, shrined within the cloud.

When we walk this mysterious journey together, present to each other and to God, it doesn't matter how "far" we go in a day because we are already "there."

In the cathedral at Chartres, France (dedicated at about the same time that this hymn was written), one chapel floor contains a large mosaic labyrinth for walking meditation. As you enter the circular tile path from the outer edge, you find that it is a remarkably long trip to the center—a trip that winds around in all directions, and sometimes seems to be leading you away from the goal. But unlike a maze with dead ends and "wrong answers," this icon of the spiritual journey provides a sure path. As long as you continue to take the next step forward, you are sure to arrive at home.

No matter what you do, stay with the questions. Who are we at a faith level? What are we here for? Who is our neighbor today? How might we reconnect faith and context in a fresh and lively way?

People of faith have discovered over the millennia that our deepest answers to these questions may take the form of stories and symbols, rather than propositions and plans. Earlier in the book, I described a demoralized and contentious downtown church that had mourned for decades over its "jewels and ashes." The members of this congregation found themselves in uproarious laughter the day a member of the planning committee offered them a parable of their current life—the 38th day on Noah's ark. She recounted in earthy detail the sights, the smells, and the disputes that must have been present after this little ecosystem had been shut up together in the ark for five rainy weeks, its occupants wondering if they would ever set foot on land again. In the act of telling a "guiding story"[2] about the church's uncomfortable present, the committee helped to evoke a new sense of human and divine companionship on a journey that seemed interminable. The storyteller's love and humor were met with laughter, recognition, and a new sense of camaraderie. I hope you will spend plenty of time finding stories and symbols that name your congregation's present reality and crystallize your vision for the future.

---

1. What difficult choices has your congregation made in the past? What themes and patterns characterize your church's way of grappling with tough questions?

2. Think of a hymn, story, or symbol that might sum up:
   a. Who/what your church was that you are no more.
   b. Who/what your church is today.
   c. Who/what your church is called to be that you are not yet.

   For each part of this question, write a sentence or two about why you selected what you did.

3. Questions 1 and 2 might lend themselves to a time of reflection at a board retreat, congregational meeting, adult group, women's guild, prayer group, or men's breakfast (or all of these). How might you invite the congregation into a season of reflection on these issues?

Seek a Partnership with Your Denomination

Many declining congregations feel frustrated that the denominational office hasn't helped them enough over the years. Many denominational staff members feel frustrated that declining congregations are either defensive (hiding data, rejecting advice, blaming denominational policies for decline) or overdependent (acting helpless, waiting for a savior, expecting automatic financial support). The great majority of denominational officials are actually quite worried about the number of declining churches in their care. In fact, they may feel as though they are drowning in a sea of congregational needs. Some spend the lion's share of each day dealing with painful crisis situations—everything from a devastating fire to sexual misconduct to a major church fight (perhaps involving a lawsuit against the denomination). Many came to their jobs with relatively little training in congregational development, conflict management, coaching, consultation skills, or leadership of systemwide change. Those with more background and bigger ideas about providing resources to congregations may feel beaten down by budget fights, staff cuts, and contentious arguments about the "right" way to save the church.

In many cases, declining congregations can take steps to establish a creative working partnership with a denominational staff member or mission department. To begin, you could:

- Gather key facts about the state of the congregation, including a list of all possible scenarios for the future you can imagine.
- Request an hour on the calendar of your bishop, executive, or area minister, or appropriate program staff member (perhaps several months from now).
- Send three or four leaders, including your pastor, to visit this person in his or her office during the day.
- Make a concise, ten-minute presentation about your situation and your possible scenarios.
- Ask this denominational leader for suggestions about books or other resources that might help you think about your situation (including both denominational programming and outside resources).
- Ask for other scenarios this leader might be able to think of, and for the names of other people who could help you expand your list of options.
- Thank your denominational staff member, and assure him or her that you will get back in touch in a few months with a briefing about what you have learned. Ask whether a letter or another visit would be best for this report-in.
- Find out more about all the suggestions and leads—even if they don't seem appealing at first. You may hit pay dirt; if not, you will at least build trust by taking your colleague's suggestions seriously. Follow through on the report-in as agreed.

I suspect that the sequence I've just outlined doesn't happen very often in our denominational offices. Congregations tend to avoid their bishop, executive, or staff until they are in a real mess. At that point, they are often pretty demanding and critical about the response they receive. On the other hand, almost everybody likes to be paid the compliment of being asked for advice—especially when you go to them on their turf, and when you make it clear that you're not expecting them to "fix it" for you.

Some shared wisdom is emerging around the church about what sort of role denominational offices can helpfully play. In his book *Transforming Congregations for the Future,* Alban Institute founder Loren Mead included these roles on his list:[3]

- *"Congregations need help when they get in trouble."* This includes severe conflict, sexual or financial misconduct, and other distressing events. In many cases, the denominational staff may refer the congregation to trustworthy external resources.
- *"Congregations need to be left alone."* Most congregations are working at ministry in a reasonably healthy way; if this is the case, the bishop or executive's office is counseled to exercise a "bias toward neglect." Generally, the best moment to offer help is when the congregation asks.
- *"Congregations need to be jacked up when they are off base."* Sometimes churches neglect their surrounding community in obvious ways, or behave in an exceptionally hostile manner toward others in the denominational family. In such cases, Mead urges denominational officials to look for some way to get a third party involved who can raise tough questions and help people "think about what they are doing."
- *"Congregations need pastoral care."* In times of catastrophe or the untimely death of a leader, or on occasions of special celebration, congregations need to feel the pastoral presence of denominational leaders.
- *"Congregations need pastoral care for their pastors."* Clergy go through times of personal and professional distress when they need to experience denominational support; Mead recommends a "bias toward health"—i.e., providing resources and challenges, not just sympathy.
- *"Congregations need help with leadership development."* Programs for clergy who are new to their congregations are especially helpful; denominations can also provide training for new church officers, and for lay leaders involved with program areas such as music, education, and youth ministry. The latter are especially helpful to the smallest churches. Congregations also appreciate referral to other training resources and scholarships for clergy and lay continuing education.
- *"Congregations need a sense of their place in the larger mission."* This is not just a question of raising the denominational mission

budget—each congregation needs a sense of participation in the church's wider work.

- *"Congregations need someone who listens and listens and listens."* In a sense, churches need to feel that they have "persistent friends" who stay in connection through thick and thin—even when there are no denominational programs to sell or set answers to give. Relationship is central.

Perhaps this list will help you clarify what you are actually seeking from your denominational staff colleagues. Since they may not have read the same book, or may have very specific priorities for their own use of time, remember that you need to discuss with these staff members what your church needs and what supporting roles they believe they can play.

---

1. In what ways have members of your denominational staff assisted your congregation in the past? (Most churches discover that the list is longer than they expected.)

2. What frustrations have you experienced as you have sought help from your denominational office? How have you and other leaders behaved when you were frustrated?

3. What kinds of help would you like from your denomination today? What steps could improve the chances that you will find (somewhere) the resources you need for effective ministry?

One controversial type of denominational help for declining congregations is funding. You may be part of a system that was accustomed to giving financial assistance to churches that could no longer pay for a full-time pastor or for building upkeep. If this was the case in the past, you have probably noticed a change in policy: Perhaps congregations have been given two to five years of diminishing support, at the end of which they are "on their own." To some extent, this move is based on financial necessity. Denominational budgets have been shrinking since the 1970s, partly because of membership loss and partly because members have a different concept of mission—as congregations recognize the "mission field" outside their own front door, they are inclined to keep more mission dollars at home.

To some extent, new policies on financial aid to congregations also arise from the conviction that long-term grants create unhealthy dependency—a belief for which there is considerable supporting evidence. Whether the money comes from the denomination's "home mission" funds or from the congregation's own endowments,[4] these grants or transfers to cover operating expenses have often discouraged congregations from facing hard truths about their circumstances. Avoiding those facts guarantees further decline. Many of the old mission-support systems had another problem as well—they tended to focus attention and resources on institutional weakness, rather than on the task of matching ministry strengths with missionary opportunities. The result was an upside-down reward system with incentives to fail.

I believe there is another side to this story, however. We live in a society where the gap between the richest and the poorest is widening steadily. We live in a time when city and suburb keep drifting farther apart. Many of us are affiliated with mainline churches whose members (by and large) had the resources to leave city neighborhoods when the fabric of civic life started to unravel. In this respect, our social context is not morally neutral.

A distinguished sociologist of race and class in America, William Julius Wilson, was recently interviewed[5] by Jim Wallis, editor of *Sojourners* magazine. When Wallis asked Wilson to explain "the stunning silence in this country about rising social inequality," Wilson replied:

> The optimistic scenario is this: As productivity grows, it creates a situation where the rising tide lifts all boats. It resembles the period from the end of World War II to about 1973, when all income groups experienced a substantial increase, even the poor. But just as we begin to become a little bit optimistic about economic growth, the press starts talking about inflation and how it's slowing down the economy. They place much more emphasis on the interests of Wall Street and the elite segment of society and have less concern about the effect of inflation on the poor. Many ignore what would be more beneficial to the masses—a full-employment-type labor market. . .
>
> Biological racism—the belief that blacks are genetically inferior to whites—has declined significantly over the years. But a

form of cultural racism has emerged in the sense that people say, "Look, we should not support poor blacks with government programs because they are in a situation because of their own personal deficiencies, their lack of a work ethic." They may not explicitly endorse the biological argument, but they do feel that blacks are responsible for the plight they are in. This is what my colleague here at Harvard, Larry Vogel, calls "laissez-faire racism."

Wilson is not talking about race alone; it has become fashionable, he reminds us, to blame and demonize a variety of vulnerable groups, including immigrants, welfare recipients, and anyone benefiting from affirmative action.

It would not be unreasonable to add certain congregations to Wilson's list—those made up of people whose "boats are not lifted" by the current tide of prosperity. While self-reliance is good (and highly valued in postcolonial churches around the world), this virtue becomes distorted to the extent that it is used to "trump" other virtues, such as justice, compassion, or shared responsibility for the church's overall mission. Saying to a congregation in a devastated community, "Be self-supporting; it's good for you," may be the spiritual equivalent of the misguided admonition, "Go in peace; keep warm and eat your fill" (James 2:15)—gratuitous advice that makes no ethical response to the person or group in dire need. I believe it is more honest for denominational leaders to say, "Our congregations are willing to offer collective support to this much missionary outreach with marginalized populations," and then to build healthy and sustainable structures of ministry to the extent those resources will allow.

In the story of St. Gabriel's, Philadelphia, I described a diocesan mission strategy that deploys full-time "urban missionaries" in eight churches. Many of these congregations are located in communities that the Percept Group would label "transformational." According to Percept literature,[6] this type of community is characterized by extremely high diversity (including racial and ethnic diversity) and extremely high population density. Such a community environment "is likely to be so dynamic that it is being transformed on a continual basis." Mary Laney said the same thing more simply when I requested written material about St. Gabriel's: "By the time I write it up, it has changed."

Particularly in these transformational settings, the central work of redevelopment—reconnecting faith and context—may not be possible for mainline denominations if complete self-support is the goal. Three decades ago, Lyle Schaller (a current critic of denominational subsidies) commented that a "pure congregational polity will eliminate the church from the inner city."[7] Reflecting on the current situation of the Episcopal Church in the Philadelphia area, John Midwood comments: "In a society like ours where neighborhoods are segregated by economic class, a regional judicatory becomes an important missionary agency. The resources to ensure that viable congregations will be found throughout a metropolitan area are located at a diocesan level." Appendix C provides sample documents from the Diocesan Coalition for Mission and Ministry (a group of congregations for which Midwood provides oversight), outlining four categories of congregations receiving developmental assistance, including diocesan missions like St. Gabriel's and new starts in growing communities.

If you are a church leader in a "transformational" type of neighborhood, you should bear in mind that denominational mission-funding schemes tend to rise and fall with political and economic tides in the larger society and in your particular denominational organization. Central support also becomes vulnerable whenever the pastoral leadership changes; your denominational system is likely to reassess its commitment when it is preparing to issue (or endorse) a new call.

Leaders in denominationally funded congregations may spend an enormous percentage of their time filling out forms, attending budget hearings, and doing enough promotion to keep their work visible in the wider system. Your congregation's morale and energy may become dangerously linked to the quality of your denomination's mission strategy at a given moment—at worst, you will come to see yourselves as victims rather than as missionary leaders. Accepting denominational funding could conceivably produce a net loss in ministry energy and sustainability; you might want to consider some of the ministry alternatives described in chapter 4. Or you may want to establish a parallel nonprofit corporation that can attract government and private funding for your work in education, housing, or economic development; since these corporations have a tendency to "spin off" over time and lose connection with the congregation, some churches specify in the new organization's by-laws that the pastor will always serve as (or appoint) the president of its governing board.

1. How has your congregation funded its ministry over the years? To what extent do you rely on endowment income to balance your annual budget? To what extent do you rely on grants or loans from your denomination, foundations, or other sources?

2. If you continue your present funding practices, where will you be in five years?

3. Suppose that denominational or foundation support were cut off. Suppose that your endowments stopped producing any income for a period of time. What would you do?

A Comprehensive Denominational Strategy

The Southeastern Pennsylvania Synod of the Evangelical Lutheran Church in America has developed an unusually well-integrated system for fostering redevelopment ministries. Though you are probably not part of this particular region and denomination, there is a great deal to be learned from the way the synod goes about its work. As you see what resources it provides, you may be able to find comparable help in your own community. You may also want to discuss this example directly with your denominational staff members, to see if they could engage in partnership with you to develop some aspect of this support system that is presently missing in your own judicatory structure.

The Southeastern Pennsylvania Synod has, over a period of years, developed an assertive approach to redevelopment ministry. (Until recently, the Rev. Claire Schenot Burkat provided staff leadership for this effort in her post as mission director.) They even take the initiative in defining what they mean by "redevelopment"—for this denominational staff, the term is reserved for a special intervention they offer to congregations "at risk" that have not yet slipped below a particular benchmark on the decline cycle. The synod focuses its redevelopment resources on churches that can still pay a full-time pastor (doing so requires a budget of at least $70,000), but whose average Sunday attendance has dropped into the 50 to 70 range. Theirs is a triage strategy. The denomination makes a real investment in congregations that undertake a full redevelopment process—a great deal of staff time; part of the cost of the system assessment described below; and about $2,000 per year for special evangelism purposes (training, a new sign, or direct mail, for example).

While churches with an attendance of more than 70 or less than 50 may still call on the synod staff for various kinds of assistance, they are not eligible for this intensive package geared to a specific set of needs. In a sense the synod staff is saying: "We can't do everything for everybody, but at the moment a congregation slips into the 'at risk' category, we can offer intensive help." While this level of assertiveness is somewhat unusual in mainline church systems, it is clearly part of the reason this strategy works.

Each spring the staff scans the list of all 180 congregations. They ask two questions: Which churches fit the "at risk" category? And which of those "at risk" churches are likely to experience a pastoral vacancy in the coming year? Churches that fit both criteria go on a preliminary list of candidates for the intensive redevelopment process. Since a total of 20 to 30 churches per year move into a pastoral transition, and since pastoral change creates a prime opportunity for transformation, this synod maximizes the power of its intervention by offering it only to churches that will be seeking a new pastor.

Once the congregation knows that its pastor is leaving, a Percept "Ministry Area Profile" is provided.[8] The congregation receives a visit from one of its denominational executives, who explains what it means to be "at risk," and inquires about the church's possible interest in the redevelopment program. The church is free to decide whether it will participate. If the congregation's leaders express initial interest, they are given the full "covenant" document for study, discussion, and questions. The complete text of this covenant is found in Appendix D. Before the redevelopment process begins, the covenant document goes to a congregational meeting for approval. Originally, synod staff would attend these meetings to provide information; now the synod has an informal speaker's bureau of lay members from other redevelopment congregations who go to churches considering the covenant to answer members' questions about the process.

One other critical step occurs before the synod offers the church a pastoral candidate. "I found out the hard way," says Claire Burkat. "You put in a really good pastor/evangelist, and then find there was already conflict or scandal in the congregation." Now, before a covenant is signed, the congregation is required to work with a team of professionals who help the congregation to "excavate"—i.e., look deeper into the human dynamics at work in its life. This work is done by an interdisciplinary firm called Physis Associates, whose staff includes psychologists, pastoral counselors, social workers, and organizational consultants. They work extensively with religious systems.

A team of three from Physis meets with a small group of people whom the congregation has selected, and together they plan the assessment work. With the Physis team, they identify individuals and natural subgroups within the congregation that should be interviewed by one of the professional facilitators. Every member of the congregation is invited to a particular group or individual interview opportunity over the course of several evenings. The team then meets to prepare a report, which describes the basic dynamics and makes specific recommendations for work that might occur over a period of months or years.

Sandra Fox O'Hara of Physis Associates says that the assessment is meant to identify "the system dynamics, the sacred cows. Some churches have lost their spiritual center because of all the power-brokering and posturing. We're trying to see whether there are enough healthy, mature people in the system to learn, reflect, and move the church ahead with hard changes. Even five can be enough of a remnant to start rebuilding a church if the pastor carefully focuses his or her attention. Our recommendations always start with the spiritual core: repentance, healing, willingness to 'come to the center.' Tweaking generally doesn't work."

In addition to recommendations for further congregational learning and communication, the report may advise that particular individuals leave their leadership positions—or even, in some cases, that the whole church council resign. The team sends the report to the council and pastor (if this person is still in place), then discusses it with them face to face. Appendix E shows a sample of a Physis report. Openness is important: The bishop or assistant attends the meeting, and the team always recommends that the report be shared subsequently with the whole congregation. This process typically costs $5,000; redevelopment congregations share this cost with the synod.

While the congregation is completing these exploratory steps, the mission director is undertaking an intensive national search for pastor/evangelist candidates. In the covenant process, the congregation has agreed to delegate to the synod the work of identifying, screening, interviewing, and recommending clergy candidates. "Looking for a redevelopment pastor," says Claire Burkat, "is the hardest thing. I've learned to be patient—I don't settle!" (Methods for identifying redevelopment pastors are found later in this chapter.) When an appropriate candidate is found, the congregation interviews the person over a weekend. The synod council issues a term call (originally three, now five years). After that, a regular call may be issued. About half of the pastors stay in place after the initial term.

This synod has worked with ten redevelopment churches over a six-year period. Claire believes that the ideal is to do this work with two or three churches at a time: "Don't start with one," she says, "because the group is important." A member of the synod staff meets with redevelopment pastors every other month, and it helps when there are several all going through the same experience.

---

1. What appeals to you about the Southeastern Pennsylvania Synod approach? What bothers you?

2. How closely do you fit its definition of an "at risk" congregation?

3. How willing would you be to accept the requirements, especially delegation of pastoral screening to denominational staff, and participation in an assessment of the human system using a team of outside professionals?

4. How might you form a partnership with your own denominational staff to find or create some of the resources the Southeastern Pennsylvania Synod provides?

Pastoral Leadership for Redevelopment Ministry

According to Kathie Bender Schwich, executive for leadership on the national staff of the Evangelical Lutheran Church in America, "only about 5 percent of rostered [i.e., professional] church leaders have the gifts and skills for the role of mission developer." In the ELCA, the term "mission developer" is applied both to pastors selected to start new congregations from scratch and to those identified to lead transformational ministries of the kind I have been describing. Schwich views transformational work as the more difficult of the two jobs. (At a national level, Lutherans use the term "transformation," not "redevelopment," in order to focus on a positive future rather than on past difficulties. This usage should not be confused with the terminology of the Percept Group introduced earlier in this chapter—Percept is talking about community demographics, not congregational process, when it talks about a "transformational" setting.)

The ELCA's Division for Outreach has a structured program for recruiting and screening mission developers. Initial nominations come from the synod level—ordinarily, pastors need at least three years of postordination experience to be considered. After a preliminary interview with a member of the synod staff, the candidate participates in a highly structured half-day screening interview.

For any congregation or denomination seeking redevelopment pastors, this "behavioral interview" is a method worth exploring. In his introduction to this technique (widely used in business), career consultant Richard S. Deems[9] explains:

> The single best predictor of a candidate's future job performance is his or her past job behavior. . . . Interviews that probe for past job behavior have been found to be more reliable than ones that focus on personality traits. . . . And hiring decisions based on actual behavior are far more accurate than those based on gut feelings.

Interviewers begin by analyzing the actual skills needed to be effective in the position. They then develop questions that will provide a candidate with opportunities to describe the use of these relevant skills in specific past situations.

Specifying key competencies and developing good questions are difficult tasks. The ELCA engaged counseling psychologist Charles R. Ridley, along with church-development specialist Robert E. Logan, to train national and synod staff members in the behavioral interviewing method. A resource kit based on this team's work—"Training for Selection Interviewing"[10]—is now available; the package includes a facilitator's guide, instructional videos,

and participant manuals. Unlike generic materials designed for business settings, this training resource is tailored for church-development situations.
Though the focus is on starting new congregations from scratch, the material is highly relevant to redevelopment ministries. Based on a job-analysis
study in 1984 and subsequent field testing, the authors provide a detailed
description of 13 competencies considered critical—a list that has been
"used with a very high degree of success in selecting and predicting effective church planters:"[11]

1. Visionizing capacity
2. Personal motivation
3. Creating ownership of ministry
4. Reaching the unchurched
5. Spousal co-operation
6. Relationship building
7. Commitment to church growth
8. Responsiveness to community
9. Utilizes giftedness of others
10. Flexibility and adaptability
11. Building group cohesiveness
12. Resilience
13. Exercising faith

(© 1998 Charles R. Ridley and Robert E. Logan)

The participant guide also includes sample questions for exploring each of
these essential capacities in an interview.[11] These two lists, plus the inter-
viewer training materials, would provide a solid starting point for your local
selection process.

Clearly, the ELCA has an extensive support system for new-start and
redevelopment ministries. Other denominational offices (presbyteries, dio-
ceses, conferences) may have developed comparable resources—such as
the capacity to do a national leadership search for a redevelopment pastor.
Even if your regional staff does not already have these capacities (or if
resources have been lost because of budget reductions in recent decades),
you can still build a relationship with a bishop, executive, deployment officer, or mission department chair who is concerned about finding good
leadership for redevelopment work. This person may be able to identify
several other churches that could benefit from the behavioral-interview

training, and help you select a facilitator to conduct a joint workshop using the Ridley-Logan package. (Invite the staff person to go through the training with you, if he or she has not already had such an opportunity—you would help the the leader to become a more effective search partner, and you would also contribute a new competency to your wider church organization.) He or she may be willing to confer with staff in adjoining regions to conduct a special search for candidates you could interview. Since the "behavioral interview" method requires considerable skill, discipline, and objectivity, it will work best when used by the denominational office as a candidate screening tool.

So far, I have been discussing pastoral leadership from the viewpoint of a congregation seeking a new pastoral leader with the right skills to help members reconnect their faith with their context. I want to broaden the discussion now to include congregations that have a pastor in place. Three basic options are available to such a church:

a. Create a clergy-lay partnership to lead a redevelopment ministry.

b. Negotiate a transition period (with a clear end date) during which the existing pastor will help lay leaders prepare the congregation for the next stage—redevelopment ministry led by a new pastor.

c. Wait until a clergy transition occurs.

While the first option may seem the simplest, it is not so easy to accomplish. For one thing, there is already a "psychological contract" between the congregation and the current pastor, an unspoken covenant that usually casts clergy in the role of "chaplain to current members." While the church board may vote for membership growth as its top priority goal, it may also punish the pastor for directing significant energy toward those who are not now members. On the other side of the coin, a pastor may feel committed to the idea of increasing the church's evangelistic outreach in the community, but lack the temperament, skills, and pastoral orientation required for this type of ministry. Remember, mission-developer types are rare among the current mainline clergy population; most members and even most clergy have never seen at close range what this job actually requires. Though more incremental types of change may not require the full "mission developer" profile, many of these qualities will still be needed for any significant program of renewal and growth.

Where some sort of ministry assessment is desired as a basis for this decision, it would be wise for the congregation and pastor to seek a mutually acceptable third party to help them create an open and fair process, and to moderate delicate conversations. If the pastor is still unclear whether he or she has the necessary gifts for redevelopment work, referral to a clergy career development center and/or participation in a "behavioral interview" process (based on the mission-developer competencies described earlier in this chapter) might be helpful.

The second option—creating a definite transition period—may work well under certain circumstances. A climate of trust and collaboration certainly helps. If members generally perceive (accurately or not) that the pastor is being forced out unfairly, the ensuing conflict may hasten rather than reverse the congregation's decline. This "phasing out" strategy will be most successful where pastors already recognize that they are not the best fit for the congregation's next developmental step, and where they see themselves as having options—another satisfying position or an attractive early-retirement package, for example. Once again, you may need a mutually trusted third party to guide the negotiation. If the agreed time frame for the pastor's departure is relatively short (less than 18 months), the congregation will need to focus on saying good-bye well and on learning all it can about the general requirements of redevelopment ministry.

If the time frame is longer—perhaps up to three years—the congregation might negotiate with the existing pastor to focus new attention on one developmental need that he or she has the right gifts to address. A pastor with excellent skills in crisis ministry might begin to train and mentor a lay visitation team. Clergy who have served as their congregation's primary ambassador to community groups might start introducing lay leaders to the people and issues they have been working with over the years. A fine educator might teach church members how to lead the new-member course or how to start home Bible-study groups. While the pastor is working on that one, clearly defined ministry goal, lay leaders can begin to study the elements of redevelopment ministry, learn about their surrounding community, and develop a team relationship with relevant denominational leaders.

If you are a pastor who now suspects that redevelopment ministry is not your cup of tea, I would encourage you to view a well-defined transition period as a positive opportunity. Taking a defensive attitude—"they have no right to make me leave"—may stimulate opposition to your ministry and make it more likely that leaders will attempt to remove you. Whether you win or lose that political battle in the short run, you will probably find that you (and the congregation) have lost a great deal in the end. On the other hand, if you can help the congregation make its transition to another kind of ministry, you may be in a better position to negotiate for what you need—to reach a certain threshold with your pension fund, maintain insurance coverage, or have enough time to conduct a thoughtful job search. In order to prevent misunderstandings, you will want to develop a written agreement with your board.

Sometimes, the best strategy for the congregation or denomination is to wait for a clergy transition—as the Southeastern Pennsylvania Synod does. Congregational leaders can begin to learn about redevelopment and to consider the connection between faith and context, even if the present situation seems to be in a holding pattern. You can work on identifying your church's norms and on creating a welcoming climate. You can begin to establish responsible, long-term practices for reviewing the congregation's life and ministry. Procedures like an annual self-assessment really start to bear fruit in the third or fourth year, as board members gain competence with the process. (Many churches use an outside leader the first time through to get the process established.) Small steps like these may start adding up to a revitalized congregation. Or they may provide the basis for a frank conversation between board and pastor about what the congregation needs next.

Let the Story Unfold

Your congregation has a life of its own. This life is interwoven with place and time, with cultural change and persistent faith, with shifting membership and a steadfast God. The work of analyzing, planning, and deciding is essential—what we intend together is part of our congregation's character and energy. But our intending is not the end (or the beginning) of the story. For all time, God has been yearning for our companionship. For all time, God has accepted our weak-kneed, shortsighted intentions as a fragrant sacrifice. Our ancestors placed symbolic portions of their work on stone altars and set them ablaze—relinquishing them entirely into the hands of a living and trustworthy God. As we complete each step of our own work as leaders, you and I are called to relinquish it into the same transforming fire—the Spirit of God.

From his prison cell in Nazi Germany, Lutheran pastor and theologian Dietrich Bonhoeffer wrote that God will make use of our failures, and even of our successes. Those weren't hollow words for him: he and others had completely failed in their plot to assassinate Adolf Hitler, and he would be hanged for this offense just days before the liberation of the prison in which he was held. He believed that God can and will bring forth out of our failures—even out of blatantly evil actions—some fruit which God is able to use redemptively. And then, with somber humor, he added the affirmation that God can use even our successes.

For a congregation, for a pastor, numerical decline often feels like utter failure. But God has lots of experience with human failures. Indeed, the offering of a broken spirit is a gift God particularly treasures. Lifting up this sacrifice is a faith task we can complete in any circumstance, right up to our final breath. May our congregations live and die in holy curiosity about what God will make of us next.

Last week I met again with six leaders from the First Congregational Church of Waverley (Belmont, Massachusetts). We had a hard time knowing what to do next. Their interim pastor is leaving in a few weeks. The dozen or so midlife members who provide all the volunteer energy are getting more and more depleted. The choir has disbanded. Some of the older members are talking about shifting their membership to another church. Members of the search committee want to know whether to start interviewing candidates.

Tim, the moderator, spoke clearly about two imperatives he is feeling—first, to provide meaningful Christian formation for the church's small collection of children and youth, and second, to keep the facility available for the many community groups that meet there. He raised the option that the members of Waverley could start attending a nearby church on Sunday mornings—a congregation with vital worship, music, and Christian education for various age groups—while Waverley's leadership continues to gather for discernment about the future.

For about three hours, the group wrestled with this option. Would the older group feel abandoned? Would this end the relationship members have with a few of the "special-needs" people in their neighborhood? Would members end up joining the neighboring church, once they had begun to feel comfortable there?

Slowly, a proposal began to emerge, built on the foundation of Tim's suggestion. The elements look like this:

- In about four weeks (around All Saints' Day), members of the congregation would lead a special Sunday service designed as a "memorial" for the church's past—a requiem for the leaders, the people, the better days, whose loss members are now grieving.

- Starting the next week, Sunday worship would be suspended at First Congregational. Members would gather each week in the church parking lot, then drive together a short distance to the neighboring church, where they would participate in worship, education, and fellowship.
- An interim pastor would be engaged for 15 to 20 hours per week to offer spiritual support for two "cell groups" of Waverley members (described below), to provide pastoral care to the elderly, and to conduct funerals as needed.
- Midlife members of the congregation would be invited over the next few weeks to covenant with each other for a two-hour "cell group" gathering each Monday night, for the following six or seven months. At least half of each meeting would be spent on spiritual nurture—prayer, Bible study, song, personal sharing. After some refreshments, group members would do business: that is, they would continue thinking about the church's future, and would perform any essential administrative tasks. (This de facto leadership group would be designated as the official board of Waverley. That way, there would be very few "extra" meetings required beyond the cell group itself.)
- Elderly members of the congregation would be invited to establish a daytime "cell group" at the church—on a weekly, biweekly, or monthly basis. This gathering would essentially be a continuation of the existing women's group and book club but might meet more often.
- After meeting for about three months, the evening cell-group members would reassess whether they have sufficient commitment to Waverley's future to call a new pastor and to start a brand-new ministry. If not, they would plan for disposition of the church's assets and would help members connect to other congregations.

Building this proposal created some energy in the group. One member reminded the others, however, that they tended to finalize decisions before they had taken time to reflect—and as a result, their decisions tended to unravel. Tim asked me what each member might do to discern the right path.

I suggested they take a minute to think of a story, hymn, or symbol that might express what they were experiencing now. After a bit of silence, one person mentioned Job's faithfulness through many trials. Another mentioned Sarah—feeling too old to produce anything new. Someone told the story of a New England church that had closed—a handful of older members

somehow obtained a key so they could "sneak in" regularly to pray together; eventually that church reopened under new leadership as an "open
and affirming" congregation (welcoming to gay and lesbian members) and
is thriving today. Tim pulled a children's Bible off the shelf, and read us the
story of "the house built on rock and the house built on sand." I encouraged
members of the group to meditate on these images in their own prayers in
coming days. We ended with prayer together.

Today I received Tim's draft of a letter to the congregation, outlining
the proposal to sojourn with another congregation on Sunday mornings while
they complete their discernment process. Here is part of that letter:

> What we currently do for our weekly worship and how we con-
> duct the business of the church drags us further into despair, and
> will in no way result in sustainable growth. We desperately need
> to find an avenue where we can gain some spiritual nourishment
> and satisfaction from Sunday worship. We need to understand
> what our capabilities for ministry are in the Waverley area. For,
> unless we have a crystal clear picture of why we gather as a
> congregation and what the ministry of that congregation is, we
> have absolutely no chance for survival.
>
> After several months, we will assess where we feel God is
> leading us. If we feel God is calling us to establish a new and
> dynamic ministry in Waverley, to which we can contribute, we will
> proceed to seek out and call a pastor who has the skill to launch
> new ministries. However, if our meetings reveal that we are not
> able to establish a new congregation at Waverley, we will begin
> exploring other options.
>
> As disturbing as that sounds, we owe it to ourselves, to those
> who went before us, and to God to make the most efficient use of
> our resources. It would be scandalous to use all of our resources
> simply to stay open for a couple more years for just a few people.
> We can use our resources, both financial and talent, to help other
> ministries. We can offer our facility to a new and growing congre-
> gation to become their home. Simply, there are many opportunities
> through which we can minister to our community. Quite frankly,
> however, these options will see the current Waverley congrega-
> tion disappear.
>
> I see a very distinct parallel between the steps we are about to
> take and the founding of the First Congregational Church of

Waverley. About 140 years ago, a small group of people began to
worship God. They understood that God was calling them to establish a ministry and a congregation in Waverley Square. We will
soon be gathering to worship God in small groups. We will be
exploring our faith to discover whether we still have a ministry to
offer in Waverley Square.

At the end of the letter, Tim attached the story he had identified at the
meeting last week—Jesus' parable of a house built on rock and a house
built on sand. He drew the text from the children's Bible he and Debbie
read to their own youngsters at home. Tim's choice expressed the great
paradox of faith that the leaders of First Congregational now face. They
are called to think, to decide, perhaps to build something new—very adult
responsibilities; at the same time, they are called to approach God with the
open and trustful hearts of little children. Even though First Congregational
doesn't have a pastor at the moment, the members are finding in their midst
new and powerful expressions of spiritual leadership. The saints of this
congregation's past—Buddy Millet, Paul Duhamel, and all the rest—would
be proud of what is happening in this little group today.

I don't know what will happen next at Waverley. If the evening cell
group gets off the ground, I don't know what they may decide—about their
own future or about the church's. If they eventually call a pastor and try to
build a brand-new ministry in Belmont, I don't know if the effort will succeed. But in that meeting last week, they were honestly struggling to connect faith with context. Out of that struggle, God will create something new.

Chapter 1

1. Various writers have described the life cycle, including sociologists Martin Saarinen and Arlin Rothauge, and consultant Robert Gallagher. While the discussion in this section draws to some extent on each of these, the diagram comes from Gallagher.

2. For an extensive discussion of size transition, see my book *The In-Between Church: Navigating Size Transitions in Congregations* (Bethesda: Alban Institute, 1998).

3. Robert T. Handy, *A History of the Churches in the United States and Canada* (Oxford, England: Clarendon Press, 1976), 210-212.

4. George D. Younger, "Not by Might Nor by Power," in Clifford J. Green. ed., *Churches, Cities and Human Community: Urban Ministry in the United States 1945-1985* (Grand Rapids: Eeerdmans, 1996), 28.

5. Mike Regele (with Mark Shulz), *Death of the Church* (Costa Mesa, Calif.: Percept Group, Inc.; and Grand Rapids: Zondervan, n.d.). This quotation is the subtitle of the book.

Chapter 2

1. Norman Faramelli, Edward Rodman, and Anne Scheibner, "Seeking to Hear and to Heed in the Cities," 101; and Robert M. Franklin, "My Soul Says Yes," 78, in Green, *Churches, Cities*.

2. Previous suburban growth had clustered along streetcar and commuter rail lines.

3. Green, *Churches, Cities,* 8.

4. Loren B. Mead summarizes the work of many researchers in *Transforming Congregations for the Future* (Bethesda: Alban Institute, 1990); see chapter 1.

5. These figures have been drawn from Eileen W. Lindner, ed., *Yearbook of American and Canadian Churches* (Nashville: Abingdon, 1951-1996), with corrections from Ida J. Smith-Williams, research services staff, Presbyterian Church (U.S.A.), Louisville. The yearbook has not reported comparable statistics from year to year for this denomination.

6. Green, *Churches, Cities,* 250.

7. Dean R. Hoge, Benton Johnson, and Donald Luidens conducted a major study of younger Presbyterian adults, published in *Vanishing Boundaries: The Religion of Mainline Baby Boomers.* (Louisville: Westminster John Knox, 1994). This work is cited by Mead in *Transforming Congregations,* 16. Carl Dudley's *Where Have All Our People Gone?* (New York: Pilgrim Press, 1979) offered an earlier assessment of the same phenomenon.

8. Mead, *Transforming Congregations,* 16.

9. The phrase "the end of Christendom" comes from Loren Mead, *The Once and Future Church* (Bethesda: Alban Institute, 1991). Discussion of the concept of marginality can be found in Alan J. Roxburgh, *The Missionary Congregation, Leadership, and Liminality* (Harrisburgh: Trinity Press International, 1997), chapter 1.

10. Douglas John Hall, "Responses to the Humiliation of the Church," *Sewanee Theological Review* 36, 4 (n.d.): 472-481. Cited from Roxburgh, *Missionary Congregation,* 5.

11. Roxburgh, *Missionary Congregation,* 6. Roxburgh argues that even marginalization is an outdated understanding, since it presupposes that the center is still *somewhere.* In a centerless world, he prefers the term *liminality* for the position of Christian communities—a place at the threshhold.

12. George Gallup, Jr., "Will the Vitality of the Churches Be the Surprise of the Next Century?" *Religion in America* (Princeton: Princeton Religious Research Center, 1996), 8.

13. George Gallup and Timothy Jones, *The Saints Among Us* (Harrisburg, Pa.: Morehouse, 1992).

14. This description of Belmont is drawn from the town's official Web site and from an unofficial site created by local resident John Bowe.

15. The demographic description of this church's community comes from its Percept demographic profile. See chapter 3 for more information about Percept profiles.

16. Alan C. Klaas and Cheryl D. Brown, *Church Membership Initiative* (Appleton, Wis.: Aid Association for Lutherans, 1993), 15.

17. Thomas J. Peters and Robert H. Waterman, Jr., *In Search of Excellence* (Boston: Warner Books, 1998).

18. To some extent, I am making cultural, generational, and clerical judgments about this congregation's behavior. At the time, such judgments prevented me from looking harder for creative ways people might express spiritual companionship. Nevertheless, I believe that a negative interaction of faith and culture, and the poverty of ritual practices, had robbed these people of their ability to stay emotionally and spiritually connected to someone they loved at a time when she needed their support.

19. Roy Oswald's recent work *Transforming Rituals* (Bethesda: Alban Institute, 1999) may help your congregation to assess and enrich its ritual inheritance.

20. White has written about this issue in the Alban publication *Lay Communiqué*.

21. Klaas and Brown, *Church Membership Initiative*, 4.

22. Klaas and Brown, *Church Membership Initiative*, 20.

23. This questionnaire draws on the work of Speed Leas and Roy Oswald in *The Inviting Church* (Bethesda: Alban Institute, 1987), and that of Alan Klaas in *Church Membership Initiative*.

24. This questionnaire may be photocopied by the reader for use with a church group without requesting specific permission from the author.

25. Much of the historical information in this section comes from material in the church's archive: the church's *Centennial Anniversary* booklet (1965), a historical sketch by Mrs. Herbert H. Jaynes on March 18, 1979 (beginning of the church's 115th year), and a briefer sketch (anonymous) prepared sometime after 1984. I have also drawn on Richard B. Betts, ed., *Newsletter: Belmont Historical Society*, June 1987.

26. Klaas and Brown, *Church Membership Initiative*, 20-21.

Chapter 3

1. Margaret Wheatley, *Leadership and the New Science* (San Francisco: Berrett-Koehler, 1992), 90-94.

2. Wheatley, *Leadership and the New Science,* 17.

3. Wheatley, *Leadership and the New Science*, 18. Wheatley is quoting from Erich Jantsch, *The Self-Organizing Universe* (Oxford, England: Pergamon Press, 1980), 7.

4. See the fine two-part article by Gil Rendle about leaders who attempt to "keep everybody happy": "On Not Fixing the Church," *Congregations* (May-June 1997 and July-August 1997).

5. Wheatley, *Leadership and the New Science,* 96.

6. The name of both the church and the community have been changed, as have details of the story.

7. Roy Oswald and Bob Friedrich, *Discerning Your Congregation's Future* (Bethesda: Alban Institute, 1996). See especially chapters 3, 4, and 5.

8. "Congregational Self Images for Social Ministry" in Carl Dudley, Jackson Carroll, and James P. Wind, eds., *Carriers of Faith* (Lousiville: Westminster John Knox, 1991). This list is cited from Carl Dudley, *Basic Steps Toward Community Ministry* (Bethesda: Alban Institute, 1991), 60.

9. Dudley, *Basic Steps,* 2-3.

10. Percept Group, Inc., 151 Kalmus Drive, Suite A 104, Costa Mesa, CA 92626. Phone (800) 442-6277.

11. Charles Olsen, *Transforming Church Boards* (Bethesda: Alban Institute, 1995); Charles Olsen and Danny Miller, *Discerning God's Will Together* (Bethesda: Alban Institute; and Nashville: The Upper Room, 1997).

Chapter 4

1. See Stewart Zabriskie, *Total Ministry: Reclaiming the Ministry of All God's People* (Bethesda: Alban Institute, 1995).

2. Lyle Schaller, "Designing a New Tomorrow for the Neighborhood Church," *Net Results,* June 1998, 14.

3. Lyle Schaller, "Reversing Decades of Numerical Decline, *Net Results,* December 1997, 13.

4. Lyle Schaller, "From Older and Smaller to Younger and Larger: The Road to Redevelopment," *Net Results,* October 1991, 6.

5. Gerald Gamm, *Urban Exodus: Why the Jews Left Boston and the Catholics Stayed* (Cambridge, Mass.: Harvard University Press, 1999), 224.

6. Gamm, *Urban Exodus,* 262. Gamm notes that the Association of Boston Urban Priests (organized in response to the riot in 1967) "challenged the church hierarchy to assume a new, more active role in dealing with the problems of poverty and racism," 264.

7. Gamm, *Urban Exodus*, 283.

8. See the discussions of Episcopal and Lutheran urban strategies in Green, *Churches, Cities.* For the Lutherans (ELCA), a foundational document in the 1980s was "The Parish as Place: Principles of Parish Ministry." The six principles are summarized by Richard Luecke in his chapter of *Churches, Cities and Human Community,* "Themes of Lutheran Urban

Ministry, 1945-85," 136-137. For a time, Forward Movement, an Episcopal tract publisher, carried Robert Gallagher's monograph "Stay in the City," which enunciated similar understandings of parish ministry.

9. Schaller, "Reversing Decades of Numerical Decline," *Net Results,* December 1997, 12.

10. *Net Results* sells an outstanding packet of reprints called "Schaller on Revitalizing Long-Established Churches." You could not make a better investment of $16. Write *Net Results* at 5001 Ave. N, Lubbock, TX 79412. Or call (806) 762-8094.

11. From *Singing the Living Tradition* (Boston: Beacon Press, 1993), © Unitarian Universalist Association, 1993; words by Mark L. Belletini; music, Czech folk tune; arrangement and text © Unitarian Universalist Association.

12. See Charles Arn, *How to Start a New Service* (Grand Rapids: Baker Books, 1997). The specific citations here are from an earlier Arn article, "Multiple Worship Services and Church Growth," *Journal of the American Society of Church Growth* 7 (1996): 73-104.

13. Arn says that seating capacity estimates must be updated with cultural change. A pew that was estimated to seat five a generation ago would now comfortably seat three, because the comfort zone has grown to 30-36 inches.

14. Arlin Rothauge, *Sizing Up a Congregation for New Member Ministry* (New York: Episcopal Church Center, n.d.). Available from Episcopal Parish Services, P.O. Box 1321, Harrisburg, PA 17105. Phone (800) 903-5544. Thse brief descriptions included here come from my book *The In-Between Church: Navigating Size Transitions in Congregations* (Bethesda: Alban Institute, 1998), 4-5.

15. Kermit L. Newkirk, "Rendell Refugees," *Philadelphia Interfaith Action,* June 1999.

16. In 1990, 19 churches had been receiving ongoing financial support. Several churches closed, and a number of others were merged or yoked.

17. Six diocesan missions were designated initially; two others were added later.

18. Zabriskie, *Total Ministry.*

19. See Arlin Rothauge's booklet, *Parallel Development: A Pathway for Exploring Change and a New Future in Congregational Life* (n.d.), from the Congregational Vitality Series, distributed by Episcopal Parish Services, P.O. Box 1321, Harrisburg, PA 17105. Phone (800) 903-5544.

Chapter 5

1. Text attributed to Thomas Aquinas; translation from *The Hymnal 1940,* © Church Pension Fund, used by permission.

2. Charles Olsen identifies storytelling and history-giving as core practices of a church board. For suggestions, see chapter 3 of Olsen's *Transforming Church Boards into Communities of Spiritual Leaders* (Bethesda: Alban Institute, 1995).

3. Loren Mead, *Transforming Congregations for the Future* (Bethesda: Alban Institute, 1994), chapter 4.

4. Once a congregation has a clear plan for redevelopment, part or all of its endowment fund may need to be used to implement the plan. Since endowment funds lend stability and resilience to ministry, other alternative funding sources should be applied first.

5. "A Coalition of Power and Hope," *Sojourners,* September-October 1999, 24-26.

6. This quotation is drawn from the standard "Study Guide" material provided in Percept's product called "Vista, Phase 1: Visioning." Such reports are provided to judicatories that contract with Percept for a comprehensive demographic analysis of their entire geographical area. I am drawing from the study guide chapter titled "THROUGH: Patterns through the Trajectories," and particularly from the section "Magnet Subtypes."

7. "Organizing for Missions," *Home Missions*, September 1970. Cited in Green, *Churches, Cities*, 214.

8. In chapter 3 of this book, see the section "Renewed Identity and Purpose" for information about Percept.

9. Richard S. Deems, *Interviewing: More than a Gut Feeling* (West Des Moines, Iowa: American Media Publishing, 1994), 8-9. This guide is accompanied by an instructional video, available from Blanchard Training and Development, phone (800) 728-6052.

10. The "Training for Selection Interviewing" kit is available for less than $200 from ChurchSmart Resources, 350 Randy Road, Suite 5, Carol Stream, IL 60188. Phone (800) 253-4276.

11. "Training for Selection Interviewing: Participant's Manual" (Carol Stream, Ill.: ChurchSmart Resources, 1998), 92-96.

12. "Training for Selection Interviewing: Participant's Manual," 104-109.

Trend Scan: The View From Here

As part of a general review and assessment process, AI asked its staff, consultants, and a variety of outside commentators to describe "the view from here." We asked them to cite the societal trends that they see affecting local congregations. Identifying those trends will help us to choose our future paths. We also hope the process will help congregations to locate themselves among the trends and to determine new courses of action.

Just as it is impossible to say exactly when a trend begins or ends, it is difficult to say exactly "where" any trend is or is moving at a given instant. So a project like this remains a work in progresss–loose, flexible, and liable to change. Nevertheless, we all need at certain points to try to "capture" a moment in time, to take a quick snapshot before the scene changes again. What follows is a list of elements that make up "the view from here" early in 1997.

Sociocultural Trends

The U.S. is moving through a period of profound change characterized by increasing social, ethnic, cultural, and religious pluralism. Individuals and groups face unprecedented and overwhelming choices and strains in patterns of living and unprecedented diversity in the people and factors shaping the context for choice. At the dawn of the 21st century, the nation has no predominant value system or model of social life with which to confront the epic changes underway. Instead, it has a variety of models that are both stimulating in their breadth and confusing in their multiplicity. These models are often in conflict with one another.

At the same time as there is no generally accepted value system, there is no widely acknowledged authority positioned to influence or advocate today's values definitively. This reflects another major factor distinguishing our period of change: a lack of trust in authority generally and a particular disenchantment with groups formerly regarded as authoritative. These include government, politicians and the political process, civic leaders, educational institutions, law enforcement, the justice system, and institutional religion.

❑ **New diversity in the population**
  • Demographically, the U.S. is becoming ever more multiracial and multicultural, with new waves of immigration deepening our nation's experience of diversity. Census data show that the percentage of the population that is **foreign-born** has almost doubled since 1970 to 8.8%; it is now at its highest level since prior to World War II. Recent increases in ethnic diversity have produced centers of new energy and vitality (including religious vitality) where, for example, Hispanics, Asians, Indians, and people from eastern Europe have recently settled, reshaping cities such as Los Angeles, New York, Minneapolis, and Chicago.
  • **There is more diversity in behavior and lifestyle** as well as in ethnic origin. The proportion of U.S. households with married couples fell by 10% in the past 25 years to 78%. Gay and lesbian households have increased. The percentage of children living with two parents went from 85% in 1970 to 73% in 1994. Primarily because of economic factors, new household groups are also increasing, composed of intergenerational or nonrelated members.
  • While the population is further diversifying, it is also aging. The median age in the U.S. is 34.5 years—the oldest it has ever been. Between 1960 and 1994, the total U.S. population grew by 45%, but the population 65 years and older grew by 100%. Currently, 13% of the population is 65 or older. Many seniors live alone for increasingly longer periods of time.
❑ **Separation of age-groups**. The growing aging group contrasts with the 26% of the population who are under 18. Young and old are sometimes described as competing for the same scarce resources. They are also separated by communicating in different "languages." Earlier generations grew up on words; younger generations—raised on TV and computers—respond more strongly to images—an entirely different "language." The future world will be an electronic one in which communication will be based primarily on images.

U.S. Foreign Born Population, 1995

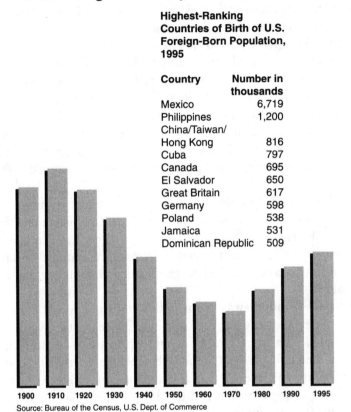

Highest-Ranking Countries of Birth of U.S. Foreign-Born Population, 1995

Country	Number in thousands
Mexico	6,719
Philippines	1,200
China/Taiwan/ Hong Kong	816
Cuba	797
Canada	695
El Salvador	650
Great Britain	617
Germany	598
Poland	538
Jamaica	531
Dominican Republic	509

1900 1910 1920 1930 1940 1950 1960 1970 1980 1990 1995

Source: Bureau of the Census, U.S. Dept. of Commerce

❑ There are **gains in racial equality and economic well-being** of African-Americans, but also **new or resurgent forms of racism** (Black church burnings) as well as attitudinal reversals on such issues as affirmative action. Hate groups have proliferated and are using technology to spread their message to more people.

❑ **Gender and sexuality issues** still figure prominently in public and church discussion. Since 1980, the percentage of women working outside the home has increased by 13%; 59% of all women over the age of 16 are in the labor force. Yet women still experience salary discrepancies with men, as well as "glass ceilings" in their efforts toward leadership advancement. **Abortion and homosexuality** influence political races and continue to affect public and church discussion. There are increasing reports of **sexual abuse** of children and sexual harassment of women. This has been a problem within churches as well as in the wider society.

❑ **Increasing globalization/increasing localism**
   • The U.S. is linked inextricably to the rest of the globe: the **global village** continues to shrink, due especially to technology. Political, economic, social, cultural, and religious forces increasingly operate across national and international boundaries. The same trends affecting North America–increased immigration and diversity–characterize other areas as well, particularly Europe. Recent epic changes such as the demise of communism and the economic rise of Asia directly affect life in the U.S.
   • While North Americans join international internet communities, they also tend to focus more on certain local realities than on the "big picture." This is due partly to mistrust of larger authorities. The very growth in power of global forces sometimes strengthens nationalism and local loyalties. Localism can be both reactionary parochialism and a sign of vital life.

❑ **A possible move away from individualism, toward community.** Some commentators say that the "self-indulgence" of the 1960s-1980s is on the wane, with more interest being expressed in relationships and groups–as well as in political agendas that include a common good. Other pundits continue to argue that radical individualism is "the" American trait, especially regarding economic realities. People desire community, but seek it in new ways. Many interest or associational groups never meet in person, but connect over the internet, for example, allowing people to create new kinds of relationships. At the same time, there has been a notable reduction in domestic civic participation. Americans join fewer groups (they go "bowling alone" in the words of political scientist Robert Putnam), participate less in civic life, and vote less than they once did.

❑ In recent decades, Americans have felt they are living in an **"uncivil society."** There is a widespread perception that human relationships–personal, professional, in business and civic life–are coarsening. Indexers at Fordham University determined that the nation's sense of social well-being has fallen to its lowest point in almost 25 years. Many of people's actions are motivated by fear. From 1974 to 1993 violent crimes, including dramatic acts of terrorism, increased 63%. Domestic violence is also widely prevalent (and widely reported), as is the teenage suicide rate, which is

95% higher than it was in 1970. On the other hand, in the past year crime has gone down. Some fears are due simply to **perception**–often based on media images. For example, New York has a lower crime rate than Minneapolis, but nevertheless exemplifies urban evil to many Americans.

Economic Trends

❑   **The market economy dominates.** The American economy is globalizing rapidly. Analysts are divided on whether the global market will produce an era of peaceful prosperity or an eventual crash. The U.S. labor force feels its rights to fair wages have eroded; it blames both foreign workers and American management. White-collar and professional workers no longer have confidence in job security. Meanwhile, the economy is growing (a gain not reflected equally in every part of society), and many people feel more well-off than they did ten years ago.

•   Areas once regarded as civic (or sometimes religious) responsibilities–education, the dispensation of justice, civic improvement–have become regarded as **commodities**, subject to market rules and descriptions. Rich school districts offer much better education than do poor school districts; in some cases, public schools have actually been taken over and run by private corporations as profit-making enterprises. "How much justice can you afford?" is a phrase heard increasingly as perceptions deepen that the court system is biased against the poor.

•   **In the U.S., the gap between rich and poor continues to grow.** It is currently greater than at any time since the end of World War II –by some estimates since the 1920s. Between 1983 and 1989, the top 20% of wealth holders received 99% of the total gain in marketable wealth. Census data show that the top 20% hold almost 47% of the nation's wealth; the next 20% hold around 23%. The lowest 60% hold about 30%. The mean income for the top 20% in 1994 was $91,000 (for the top 5% it was almost $141,000); for the lowest 20% it was a little below $8,000. The Fordham study concluded that in the mid-1990s, the gap worsened more quickly than any other problem except food stamp coverage. Access of the privileged to expensive technology (in medicine and communication, for example) increases the gap between rich and poor.

• **Religion**, too, is subject to market impact, as churches struggle to dispense fair wages and benefits, buy or construct buildings, pay legal costs, balance domestic and international needs, and take on increasing social service responsibilities. Religion is perceived in market terms: it is a commodity for which people "shop" and to which they feel a commitment only as long as it "serves their needs." Religious groups use market techniques to communicate their message.

Education and Training

❏ **Technological change has made education an elitist commodity.** The pervasive dominance of computers and technology has contributed to making education uneven and unequal. Job success today usually requires some knowledge of computers, but many poor school districts (let alone individuals) are still without them. In 1993, 35.8% of white youth had access to a computer, while only 13% of black youth and 12% of Hispanic youth did. Those left behind in the race for techno-skills must compete with unskilled labor around the world for low wages.

On the other hand, more high school graduates are going to college. And more people are graduating from college than in the past.

Science and Technology

❏ **More data, less wisdom?** There is a proliferation of far more data than the society at large can process or understand. But turning data into wisdom remains an ongoing challenge. Science retains an aura of mystery, and we rely on its experts (although the use of obscure and anti-rational thought is also common). On the other hand, as basic technological knowledge spreads, so do dangers ranging from homemade bombs to the capability to invade government, business, and personal computers.

• **Increasing numbers of people recognize a need to protect the earth.** In last fall's elections, environmental legislation in states generally passed. The government may challenge industry and commerce toward tighter controls. There are new partnerships working to improve the situation; for example, the Union of Concerned Scientists is producing educational materials in cooperation with the National Religious Partnership for the Environment.

- At the same time, there is still much confusion about "scientific proof" for many basic problems. For example, one position states that smoking definitely causes cancer, while another position says there is no scientific proof of cause and effect. On the global front, **population explosion** continues to strain natural resources. But some people do not consider population growth an addressable "environmental" issue like recycling or industrial pollution, especially when its effects seem so far away.

- A number of new books bring **science and religion closer together**, as scientists find religious ideas increasingly compatible with the scientific discoveries about the origins of the universe. People look to science for help with ethical issues such as artificial life-support, genetic engineering, or defining the moment of death.

Religious Realities

American society displays a strong interest in religion, and many commentators have written of widespread spiritual hunger. People still look to religion for **meaning and values**. However, many of them look less to religion for **authority** than they once did. Seekers seem more interested in spirituality than in religion, especially institutional religion, and most especially, mainline religion. But other people seek strong authority in organized religion: around the world, all major faiths have seen the rise of fundamentalisms. In the U.S., most fundamentalist and evangelical churches have grown or maintained membership.

Changes in attitudes about authority and leadership coincide with changes in how information is disseminated and how people want it to be disseminated—both within the church and in the wider world. During the age of Christian/Protestant dominance, means of communication and authority suggested a solid image like a building—perhaps like the Athenian Parthenon. An overall roof of Christian values, ideas, and goals was supported by numerous vertical columns, each representing a denomination or communion. Information and authority flowed vertically form the roof down the columns, while each column remained separate and distinct as well, containing its own particular ethos and identity.

The situation is different today. Instead of an image of a building, another type of image—such as a web—may be more appropriate. In a web there is not just one way to receive information, ideas, or leadership. Rather, parts of the web are connected in various ways that allow communication to move horizontally, vertically, diagonally, or in various paths. These general changes in ways of describing communication and social interaction underlie all of the many other ways in which parts of the religious world are changing.

❑ **Congregations are changing.**

• Membership in the mainline is **aging**. It has also generally been losing members for some time. Participation and financial support have also been declining. Mainline congregations need to serve both long-time members and newer, younger members, who have **different expectations**. As a result of these pressures, some congregations are engaging in experiments with new models of ministry, such as megachurches, "alternative" services, evening services, and so on. Other congregations are attempting to hold fast to earlier models.

• Parishioners express a desire for a more intense feeling of **community**, yet they have difficulty defining or finding exactly what they mean. Small groups have been a major effort to address this need in congregations.

• **Teen-agers and young adults** seem disconnected from mainline congregational life. There have now been several generations of biblically illiterate youth, and even those within the churches are not necessarily trained in the basics of the faith or the denomination. Major efforts to revamp youth programs are underway.

• Some observers see an increasing sense of tension and **conflict** between clergy and laity. This may arise around **financial issues**, issues of **authority**, or other matters. When problems do occur, they often seem a result of confusion and lack of understanding. For example, in the financial area, laity and clergy may not have the same understanding of the financial resources a pastor needs. Because new leadership models are emerging for both clergy and laity, it may be unclear who has **authority** to make a particular decision or organize a congregational ministry program.

• **Finances** are a huge concern for congregations—with some falling below the minimum level to continue operations. Yet there are also creative new movements such as coalitions, church-to-church loan programs, or organizations of endowed churches seeking cooperation and mutual advice to address the economic needs of their own and other congregations.

Congregations are undoubtedly here to stay. As religious people continue to focus locally, the local church will remain primary. However, congregations may dramatically change shape. They may merge into denominational clusters, become ecumenical congregations, hire several part-time clergy, increase lay ministry, offer radically new types of services, or reprogram their ministries to reflect the aging of their members. Observers such as sociologist of religion Nancy Ammerman argue that perhaps more than anything else, congregations are shaped by—and must take account of—member **transience and movement**.

❏ **Denominations have shrunk**. Mainline denominations struggle with issues of diversity and identity. Signs of major change have abounded: membership loss, downsizing, restructuring, decline in financial well-being.

• Members of local congregations have only a vague notion of what a denominational headquarters does. Denominational leaders are buffeted by criticism from every direction. Many are searching for new understanding of what it means to be a denomination in late-modern America. Some would interpret these trends as a breakdown; others as an indication that religious faith may be moving out of a bureaucratic age back to its roots in small, local groups.

• **Denominational identity** is not a major concern of many congregations. Denominational barriers are increasingly permeable, with church choice for many people based on factors like location or style rather than denomination. Many local congregations seem to practice a sort of natural ecumenism. Some analysts would say that this is not a "real" **ecumenism** because it has not developed out of deep theological conversations; others, taking a more experiential approach, affirm the validity of this sort of ecumenism. Congregations wishing to be ecumenical are searching for resources.

Interest groups and networks exist across denominations. These often form around social, political, or personal-lifestyle issues. Examples include the "green movement," groups focusing on women's issues, and groups based on sexual affinity or attitudes toward abortion.

Bilateral and more broadly based talks between and among denominations are bringing them closer together. There has been **interfaith cooperation** on such concerns as the environment and aid for refugees.

The role of **middle judicatories** is evolving. Decline in finances and increase in local congregational focus are giving rise to redefinition of judicatory roles. Leaders are experiencing a loss of morale as they deal with cutbacks in resources and increased competition among resource providers. But there is also energetic experimentation going forward to revision judicatory roles, for example, moving away from programmatic focus to other supporting and coordinating activitities.

❑ **Clergy roles are evolving.**

• The **place of clergy** in the society and in the congregation continues to change. In addition to role confusion, there is the general loss of esteem that has affected many former authority figures. Yet many older or second-career people feel called to ministry, to which they bring gifts of experience and wisdom. In general, clergy leadership in the mainline mirrors the aging of its laity. If the enrollment of older persons in seminary is not balanced with an increase in younger seminarians, the mainline will have problems in future years with inadequate numbers of clergy.

• The entry of **women** into ministry is changing its face forever. In 1972, 10% of seminarians were women; in 1993, 31%. Women have brought creative new leadership styles to the church. Yet they still occupy few top positions in "tall steeple" churches or in denominations.

• **Seminary education** is also changing. Theological schools are beginning to require a pre-entry level of basic church knowledge, are expanding programs such as off-site learning, and are introducing new recruitment plans to attract younger students. They are also making spirituality a more central part of the educational experience, a focus encouraged in new accreditation standards adopted by the Association of Theological Schools. Some seminaries are working more in groups or clusters to avoid duplication of offerings and resources.

❑ **Laity are searching.**

• Laypeople, especially women, says sociologist of religion Wade Clark Roof, are filling new leadership roles and introducing new concerns, such as holistic health and increased integration of faith and life, into congregational awareness. There is confusion as new styles of leadership develop. Both clergy and laity need resources to help them define their respective roles.

• Laity are searching for connections to other types of resources they want, especially in areas of spirituality. They often turn to "new religions" while unaware that resources exist within their own faith tradition.

Conclusion

It is appropriate to end this scan with a reference to searching. We are all searching, really. What we find depends on how we search. The U.S., along with the rest of the world, stands not only on the brink of a new century, but on the brink of an era during which reshaping of identities will predominate. The many seemingly contradictory movements and trends cited here suggest the many alternatives for that reshaping process.

People do not want pat solutions; they want to find answers in creative combinations. More choice is required—but more options are available. This transitional time offers a unique opportunity for close re-examination of mission—what we might call "mission in movement." This is as true for the Alban Institute as it is for the congregations, groups, organizations, judicatories, and denominations that it serves.

What Happens Between Sizes?

from *The In-Between Church* by Alice Mann

Fault Lines

My brother used to live near the San Andreas fault in California. This is a long rift in the earth's crust that periodically tears open to accommodate shifts in the two tectonic plates whose meeting creates a fault line. As a visitor to my brother's home, I used to imagine myself standing with one foot on each side of the fault, then dropping into a chasm when the earthquake hit.

Size transition is a lot like standing on the fault line. You can make better decisions if you know not only where the rifts occur but also what deeper movements of the earth are driving the surface eruption. Congregations are changing and adjusting all the time. Dozens of different factors are in play, and subtle gradations exist that make any size theory look oversimplified. Still, some of the forces at work are more powerful than others, more determinative of relationships and results. For the majority of congregations,[1] a two-dimensional model of size change will clarify the lines of demarcation.

One dimension of change, shown along the bottom of the following chart, is described by the terms *organism* and *organization*. The other dimension is described by the terms *pastor-centered* and *group-centered*. Churches moving through the plateau zones on the graphs in the last chapter are actually crossing fault lines on this topographical map. As congregations move among Rothauge's four sizes—family, pastoral, program, and corporate—they follow an N-shaped path across the fault lines.

Size Transition "N-Curve"

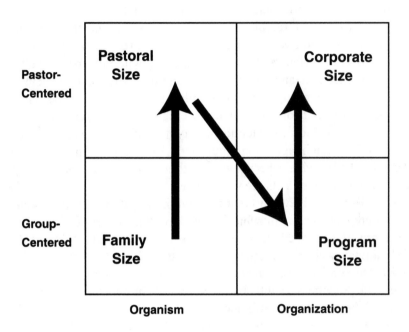

Organism   Organization

Organism versus Organization

Family and pastoral size churches resemble an organism more than an organization. Congregations of these two sizes tend to be relatively homogeneous in make-up. Each revolves around a central relationship that can be immediately and intuitively apprehended: the relationship among members as a "primary group" or "single cell" (family size church) or the dyadic relationship between the sole ordained leader and the congregation (pastoral size church). The congregation's identity is largely inherent in these central relationships. Ask the question "Who are you as a church?" in a family size congregation, and someone will probably introduce you around the whole circle of members. Ask that question in a pastoral size church, and someone will most likely tell you about the congregation's relationship with its pastor, often symbolized by the rapport (or lack thereof) between pastor and board. In these two smaller sizes, the notion that a congregation might choose or shape an identity intentionally would probably seem odd; identity is more of a given, to be preserved and defended.

In program and corporate size churches, on the other hand, the variety and complexity of relationships require conscious attention to matters of identity, purpose, structure, role of leaders, and so on. Neither the members nor the pastor can intuitively grasp the wholeness of the system. The larger membership and the rich variety of programming will only cohere well if leaders construct a clear identity for the church—often expressed in a mission statement, a vision, or a strategic plan. For people raised in smaller churches, this work of construction may seem taxing and bureaucratic. On the other hand, the quest for intentionality typical of a larger congregation might stimulate their imagination about church life, clarify their reasons for participation, and provide richer networks of friendship, growth, and ministry. Membership is more of a choice than a given.

The distinction between organism and organization is not absolute. Small congregations are still subject to the laws that govern not-for-profit corporations in the United States and may be vulnerable to lawsuits if they do not attend well to organizational matters like the employment, accountability, and termination of staff. Larger congregations are still living systems, held together by subtly balanced forces which we may only dimly perceive. Nevertheless, the difference between the two emphases is usually palpable.

Group-Centered versus Pastor-Centered

The movement from family to pastoral size (the upward arrow on the left-hand side of the chart on page 139) involves a change in the way the system centers its life. The family size church feels like a tribe or a committee of the whole. Not everyone on the committee has equal influence, to be sure, but the single cell of members works things through in its own characteristic way. A student minister or part-time pastor who tries to take charge of that cell is in for a rude awakening because a family size church does not generally revolve around the pastor.[2]

At a worship attendance of about 35 people, that single cell of membership becomes stretched. By the time it hits 50, the unbroken circle of members—that defining constellation of the congregation's life—is in crisis. In order to increase further, the system must allow itself to become a multi-cell organism, holding together two or three overlapping networks of family and fellowship. And it must establish a symbolic center around which those multiple cells can orient themselves. Typically, it becomes pastor-centered.

A great deal has been written about the dangers of clerical domination in churches, and many have questioned whether this shift to a pastor-centered system is desirable at all. I would not equate "pastor-centered" with "pastor-dominated." The research of Speed Leas and George Parsons suggests that a greater proportion of members may actually participate in decisions at pastoral size than at family size.[3] It may be that the heightened role of the pastor in relation to the board moves the congregation's political center from the kitchen table to a more accessible public setting and requires that the ordained and elected leaders work as a team to move projects forward. The pastor's central position as communication switchboard also allows for a great deal of informal consultation and problem solving; he or she can monitor key relationships, initiate needed conversations, and anticipate likely clashes.

As attendance approaches 150, however, the congregation must become more group-centered once again because the pastor can no longer carry around the whole system in his or her head. There are too many individual, pastoral needs to track. The relationships among projects and leaders are becoming too complex to be coordinated solely through board discussion and pastoral diplomacy. A new kind of teamwork becomes necessary in an uneven leadership matrix in which some programs have paid staff, some have volunteer leaders so dedicated that they function like staff, and some have committees at the helm. Board and pastor must find ways to keep the parts connected with each other *directly*—in horizontal networks of collaboration—not just *indirectly* through board reports and liaisons. As in a spider web, the center of this leadership network does not consist of a single point (the pastor) but of a small circle (half a dozen key program leaders–paid and unpaid, clergy and lay) led by the pastor.

In the move to program size, clergy must shift a good deal of their time and attention away from the direct delivery of pastoral care and focus on assembling and guiding that small team of program leaders. They must also find ways to offer spiritual enrichment to the board, whose job has become much more demanding. Skills for this kind of group-oriented ministerial leadership have not usually been emphasized in seminary or employed as primary selection criteria in the ordination process. Hence, many clergy find themselves poorly equipped for a pastoral-to-program transition.

To make things worse, the breakdown of the pastor-centered way of being a church occurs at the same time as the shift from organism to organization. The congregation is now traversing the diagonal portion of the N-shaped path, crossing both the horizontal and vertical fault lines simultaneously. The pastoral-to-program change is doubly discontinuous.

When attendance reaches about 350, the need for more pastor-centered leadership emerges once again. (Note the vertical line on the right-hand side of the chart.) The program church's lively but lumpy network of staff, volunteer program heads, and committees can no longer provide the overview and strategic direction the system needs. At corporate size, complex networks of coordination are still required, but the central pastor must begin to project a large enough symbolic presence—through preaching, presiding, leading the board, and heading the expanded staff—to unify a diverse and energetic community. To be effective, this high-profile leader must find a reliable way to maintain spiritual perspective and must use the aura of headship to help the whole system grapple with its core identity and purpose.

Six Transitions

It may be helpful to summarize some critical issues that must be addressed during the six possible transitions within the Rothauge framework. The placement of each movement on the N-curve is shown.

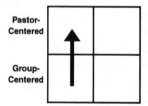

Family-to-Pastoral Transition

- Loss of self-esteem by matriarchs and patriarchs as they lose decisive influence in the system: Can they be helped to pass the mantle, with pride in the past during which they presided?
- Tendency for unseasoned clergy to take resistance personally: How can congregations find mature pastoral leadership? How can less experienced clergy find mentors to help them handle their own insecurities?

- Reluctance to divide the single cell: How can current leadership weigh what may be gained and lost as they relinquish the expectation that every event (Sunday worship, study programs, Christmas Eve service) must include the whole family?

- Financial realism: Clergy salaries and benefits are rising in most denominations. Can the congregation move solidly enough into pastoral size to attain stability?

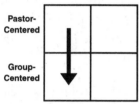

Pastoral-to-Family Transition

- Loss of self-esteem by congregation when it feels it is no longer operating like a "real" church: Will the move signal slow death, or will something new and vigorous begin?

- Ministry development: How will gifts be discerned and developed for a rich variety of home-grown ministries?

- Support and accountability: How will the family size church partner with its denomination (or with parachurch organizations) to monitor the development of sound ministries and open channels to other congregations, leaders, and ideas?

- Physical plant: What is an appropriate facility for this church? Does worship need to be moved so that the space will be at least half full on Sunday (the minimum required to attract newcomers)?

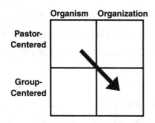

Pastoral-to-Program Transition

- Clergy role: Will leaders recognize the double messages they are giving the clergy about what they expect? (Try the "A-B" exercise in Roy Oswald's article.) Will clergy work on resolving their personal ambivalence about these choices and on gaining the new skills they need? How will staff be augmented to allow for growth?

- Program leadership: How will gifted and motivated people be selected, equipped, and authorized to serve as department heads? Does the pastor have the skills needed to forge these heads into a staff team? Who will help the average member identify gifts for ministry (inside and outside the congregation), and who will make sure that every form of volunteer service to the congregation is a spiritually rewarding experience?

- Communication: How can people involved in implementing different programs stay personally connected with leaders from other programs? Will formal information channels (newsletter, bulletin, spoken announcements, telephone trees) be improved and intensified, so that timely, accurate, and thorough communication is the norm?

- Democratic participation: What channels will be provided so that every member can have a say and a stake in the shape of church life? How will members remain aware of, and accountable to, a central purpose?

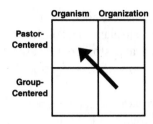

Program-to-Pastoral Transition

- Reshaping expectations: How will the congregation refocus on a few central strengths? Will there be attention to the sense of loss and grief that may accompany a consolidation of energies?

- Clergy role: What satisfactions and status must the pastor relinquish? How will simpler patterns of pastoral care be established?

- Sunday morning: How can the worship and education schedule be made manageable without reinforcing a cycle of decline? Can the church maintain at least two worship options of somewhat different styles?

- Ministry development: Healthy pastoral size churches still foster active lay leadership, especially in new-member incorporation, education, and community outreach. How will the pastor shift to a less formal style of delegation and mentoring? How will the number of committees be reduced in favor of small, hands-on ministry teams?

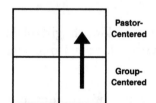

Program-to-Corporate Transition

- Depth and quality of programming: How will the church step up to a higher level of expectations? Do staff members need new position descriptions (focused on empowering others for ministry) and a definite plan to gain new skills?

- Symbolic presence of central pastor: Is the senior minister ready to step into a lonelier, more spiritually hazardous role? Will he or she put in place new disciplines such as regular spiritual guidance, adequate time for sermon preparation, and use of third-party help in planning, conflict, and staff development? Who will mentor the central pastor around new and difficult responsibilities (personnel issues, endowment, delegation)?

- Strategic direction: In a system as hard to turn as an ocean liner, how will senior pastor and central board keep their focus on the big questions about the church's purpose and role? How will they engage the rest of the system in those questions without abdicating leadership?

- Small group connection: Will the congregation establish an excellent pattern of small group ministry through which members can connect faith with daily life? Will small group leaders be trained through apprenticeship so that the more experienced leaders can constantly be forming new groups?

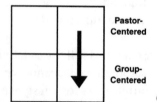

Corporate-to-Program Transition

- Relinquishing status: Will the church be honest about its decline and resist the temptation simply to keep up appearances?

- Use of endowment: Is the church steadily spending down the gifts of the past, rather than facing the need to consolidate programs and to develop a relevant approach to evangelism?

- Cavernous buildings: Does the sea of empty seats reinforce the cycle of decline and undermine the vitality that could be developed?

- Clergy role: Can the central pastor establish a more collegial relationship with the major program leaders and help the board to take back the spiritual leadership which may have been relinquished in the past to a small group of trustees?

In the case of impending transition to a smaller size, each congregation will need to assess its growth potential and outreach commitments. Don't reconfigure for the smaller size if you intend to move through the plateau zone within the next couple of years.

The Double-Minded Church

A classic prayer asks for the grace to love and serve God "with gladness and singleness of heart." Both joy and single-mindedness start to run short in a size transition; they are replaced by profound ambivalence. Once a church has entered the plateau zone, the strength and appeal of the previous size are already compromised, while the virtues of the next size are not yet in place. Leaders find themselves in a lose-lose position because two competing sets of expectations are laid upon them. Confusion, anxiety, and indecision often result.

Some of the most poignant passages in Exodus and Numbers describe the ambivalence of the faith community in its transition from the land of bondage to the land of promise. When the people first left Egypt, they were so daunted by their transitional circumstances that some of them wished aloud, "If only we had died by the hand of the Lord in the land of Egypt, when we sat by the fleshpots and ate our fill of bread" (Exod. 16:3).

Once they had received the Law and moved on from Sinai, they even began to remember *Egypt* as a place flowing with milk and honey—a description usually reserved for the promised land. Their attention constantly drifted from God's mighty acts to the most domestic of details: "We remember the fish we used to eat in Egypt for nothing, the cucumbers, the melons, the leeks, the onions, and the garlic; but now our strength is dried up, and there is nothing at all but this manna to look at" (Num. 11:5-6).

In the next chapter we will look more at questions of ambivalence and discernment, but the following Biblical Reflection questions may help you get in touch with your own inner conflicts about size transition.

Diocesan Coalition for Mission and Ministry Guidelines

Episcopal Diocese of Pennsylvania

I. Diocesan Missions

Strategic Consideration:
There are areas of the diocese where the Episcopal Church must continue its mission and ministry. Substantial diocesan resources are necessary to keep the mission and ministry viable.

Description of Congregation:
- located in "changed" or "changing" neighborhood
- longtime commitment to and history in neighborhood
- physical plant is old, requiring substantial funds to operate and maintain

Diocesan Commitment:
- pay all costs of full-time priestly ministry (salary, housing, utilities, pension, health/life insurance) directly from Church House using DCMM funds
- limited help with capital repairs from diocesan maintenance funds
- help in finding program funds from a variety of sources

Congregation's Responsibilities:
- cost of operating physical plant
- cost of parish program and operations
- full support of minimum diocesan asking

Expectations:
- congregation has a three to five year plan for its mission and ministry, including stewardship and evangelism plan

- quality ministry in congregation and neighborhood
- gradual growth in worship attendance and financial giving
- long term support by diocese

Diocesan Financial Support:
Cost of full-time priestly ministry

II. New Missions

Strategic Consideration:
In growing areas, the diocese has a responsibility to start new congregations.

Description of Congregation:
- located in rapidly growing community
- starts with an organizing pastor and a core group of lay people
- grows faster than the community

Diocesan Commitment:
- support total cost of priestly ministry initially
- diocesan support for priestly ministry decreases over the years
- help with acquiring land and buildings using resources available locally and nationally

Congregation's Responsibilities:
- program and operating expenses after two years
- gradual taking over of expenses of priestly ministry
- self-support in 5 to 7 years
- full support of minimum diocesan asking

Expectations:
- a three to five year plan for ministry
- building program within five years, including local capital fund drive
- incorporation within ten years

Diocesan Financial Support:
Full support initially, decreases after three years, none after five to seven years.

III. Congregations Receiving Diocesan Grant

Strategic Consideration:
A limited amount of diocesan aid significantly improves the mission and ministry of a congregation.

Description of Congregation:
• circumstances make congregation unable to meet combined costs of full-time priestly ministry, physical plant, parish operations and program

Diocesan Commitment:
• a grant from DCMM funds for general parish operations after congregation has demonstrated its ability to support at least half-time priestly ministry
• possible help with capital repairs from diocesan maintenance funds
• help in obtaining program and capital funds from various sources

Congregation's Responsibilities:
• operating and maintaining safe physical plant
• faithful parish ministry
• full support of minimum diocesan asking

Expectations:
• congregation has a three to five year plan for its mission and ministry, including stewardship and evangelism plan
• diocesan funding helps congregation meet its goals

Diocesan Financial Support:
Grant for general parish operations

IV. Congregations Not Receiving Diocesan Grant

Strategic Consideration:
Congregations which are able to meet the costs of at least half time priestly ministry, costs of operating and maintaining their physical plant, and cost of parish operations and program will be encouraged to do so.

Description of Congregation:
- buildings are in reasonably good order
- congregation is in reasonably good health

Diocesan Commitment:
- limited maintenance funds possible
- resources of diocesan staff available

Congregational Responsibilities:
- all expenses of congregation
- maintain at least half time priestly ministry

Expectations:
- congregation has a three to five year plan for its mission and ministry
- some growth in worship attendance, membership, stewardship
- congregation giving at least diocesan minimum diocesan asking or making progress toward meeting minimum asking

NOTE: Congregation will be referred to Mission Strategy Commission if unable to maintain half-time priestly ministry.

Used with permission of The Venerable John Midwood, Archdeacon, Episcopal Diocese of Pennsylvania.

Expectations and Responsibilities of a Pastor/Congregation under the Synodical Appointment Process for Redevelopment

Southeastern Pennsylvania Synod
Evangelical Lutheran Church in America

PREAMBLE: As the redevelopment of this congregation begins, it is essential that the partnership and the accountability structure be clearly understood by all parties. The active participants are the CONGREGATION (represented by the church council), SYNOD (through the bishop, staff person and mission director) and the PASTOR/REDEVELOPER.

PART ONE – Term of the Call and Subsequent Call

The Call to serve as pastor/redeveloper of this congregation comes from the Synod Council of the Southeastern Pennsylvania Synod of the ECLA (with the advice and consent of the congregation). The call is extended for a term of three years. During the term of the call the synod will conduct annual ministry reviews with the pastor and the congregation council. At the conclusion of third year of the term call, with the consent of the bishop, the pastor, and the congregation council, the pastor/redeveloper may be called by the congregation to serve as pastor.

PART TWO – Basic Expectations of the Pastor

The primary role of the pastor/redeveloper (in addition to being preacher/teacher and spiritual leader) is that of evangelist. It is expected that 50% of the pastor's time will be dedicated to the task of evangelization, which includes both visitation, incorporation, faith formation for the new Christians, and training of the laity for the shared task of evangelization.

The pastor/redeveloper and lay leaders are to participate in a minimum of two Evangelization Conferences during the three-year term.

The pastor/redeveloper will be responsible for the following:

a)   cultivating a hospitable climate for growth,

b)   making creative use of worship services for the purpose of inviting new members to the congregation, and adding services as needed to maximize outreach,

c)   developing, in consultation with the Mission Director and the Council, a five-year vision for church growth with significant increase in worship attendance,

d)   filing reports with the Mission Director and the congregation council.

PART THREE – Basic Expectations of the Congregation

The congregation has committed itself to a program of intentional growth in worship attendance and financial support. With the clear understanding that 50% of the pastor's time will be given to the task of evangelization, the members of the congregation will be partners with the pastor/redeveloper in this new ministry. That partnership is expressed by a commitment to:

a)   provide adequate salary and benefits to the pastor and family,

b)   relieve the pastor of excessive committee meetings with the exception of the regular monthly council meetings, and other significant meetings as determined by the laity and clergy leadership,

c)   provide specific prayer, support, and programs that directly encourage the work of evangelization,

d)   provide for the routine administrative tasks of the congregation,

e)   change the existing ministries and programs as suggested by the pastor/redeveloper in order that redevelopment of the mission of the congregation can take place,

f) provide quarterly reports from the president of the congregation council,

g) review and if necessary revise the present mission statement of the congregation,

h) share in visitation of the prospective new members identified by the pastor and congregational members,

i) in conjunction with the pastor, develop a five year vision for church growth.

PART FOUR – Basic Expectations of the Synod

The synod commits itself and its resources to supporting the congregation's redevelopment efforts through the following:

a) identify, screen, interview, and recommend pastors to serve as pastor/redeveloper. Persons so identified and recommended will have the gifts, skills, and proven experience in revitalizing and redeveloping congregations.

b) assisting congregations as needed with financial support to the extent available to the synod to enable redevelopment,

c) mission director will meet at least quarterly with the pastor/redeveloper,

d) conduct an annual ministry review with pastor and congregation council.

PART FIVE – The Support of the Pastor and Family

As noted above, it is the responsibility of the congregation to provide adequate and just compensation to the person serving as PASTOR/REDEVELOPER of this congregation. Therefore, attached to this agreement is a four-year budget projection indicating the extent of the financial support given to the pastor's compensation package.

Also attached to this agreement are the statements of salary, allowances, and benefits proposed for the initial year of the term call.

_____   _____

Bishop   Congregation Council President

_____   _____

Mission Director   Pastor/Redeveloper

                                          _____

                                          Date

Redevelopment Expectations

BISHOP

>Letter of Call
>Three-year term call

PASTOR

>First months
>Visiting congregation members
>Building relationships
>Attend Evangelization Conference
>Monthly reports first six months
>Share evangelization plan with Mission Director and congregation
>Initial calling and/or direct mail campaign in ministry area
>Develop brochure
>50% - 50% time responsibilities

MISSION DIRECTOR

>Meet initially with council
>Coordinate Evengelization training for pastor and people
>At least four times a year gather pastors
>Review pastor's reports
>Provide evangelization resources as needed
>Provide demographic assistance

SYNOD STAFF

>Once a year visit with council
>Maintain supportive contact with pastor, Mission Director,
>   and congregation

COUNCIL AND KEY LEADER

>Financial projection – salary projection (4 years)
>Attend retreat with Mission Director/or other Pastor Evangelist
>Support pastor in ministry
>Develop 5-year plan for mission

Explore evangelization possibilities for congregation
Share visitation of prospective members
Help with faith formation of new members

REVIEW OF REDEVELOPMENT MINISTRY
Annual ministry review that includes:
Pastor
Council
Representatives from Mission Development Committee
Plans/goals/finances/mission statement
Mission Directors

Used with permission.

Collaborative Development Report
Physis Associates

The "Collaborative Development Reports" prepared by Physis Associates for individual congregations are written for those people directly involved in the situation, not for general publication. Sandra Fox O'Hara has created a fictionalized report to provide you with an idea of what such a report might look like.

Collaborative Development Report
Physis Associates

NAME OF CHURCH: St. James Church
ADDRESS: 1520 Ferry Avenue
                       Columbus, OH

CONGREGATIONAL
VICE PRESIDENT: Susan Simpson

PHYSIS TEAM: Sandra Fox O'Hara
                       Cynthia Lestyk

INTERVIEWING SESSION: April 8, 1999   Three Congregational
                                            Focus Groups
                                            Church Council

INDIVIDUAL
INTERVIEW: April 17, 1999   Pastor Donald Landis

FEEDBACK SESSION: April 30, 1999   Church Council
                                    Rev. Lamont Sperry,
                                    Assistant to the
                                    Bishop

Process Observations

The atmosphere at St. James Church on Ferry Avenue was one of empti-
ness and depression. With each visit, the climate in the church was clearly
one of giving up and discouragement. The church building is barely utilized
other than for worship, as there is virtually no programming.

Paradoxically, during the focus groups, a community choir rehearsed.
The backdrop to the conflict-ridden focus groups was the community choir
energetically singing "Give My Regards to Broadway" and "I'm Going to
Wash That Man Right Out of My Hair" with life and vigor. The contrast to
the sense of impending demise was glaring, and the metaphor of having
recently voted to terminate a pastor was evident.

The members were divided by the council as the "yes" people and the
"no" people–the "yes" being those who voted yes for Pastor Landis, and
the "no," those who voted against. In every discussion, people were cast
into those categories. There was no cohesive congregation to discuss.

Historical Dynamics

The history at St. James Church is laden with conflict between a subgroup
of members and the former pastors. From the 1950s on it was reported that
pastors who tried to make changes (particularly bringing in members of the
community) were resisted by a subgroup of the congregation who wanted
to keep the status quo. It was also reported that the men of the church
had for many years been primarily responsible for its functioning; once in
those roles, these lay leaders resisted rostered leadership and saw it as an
attempt to diminish their control.

The situation of powerful members being in control reached critical
proportions during Pastor Landis's ministry in that members refused to dis-
close financial information, inform others where important records were
kept, or cooperate with an outside financial audit. Pastor Landis pursued

the audit and during his administration brought the church into financial accountability. Financial investments keep the congregation in operation today. St. James Church is not solvent in that current income does not support operations.

Many people report that they do not know the reasons each former pastor left. Although each gave a reason (moving onward and seeking new challenges), many members of the congregation wondered if a particular subgroup had not driven out one pastor after the other. In the last several years, the power struggle has become more public. The leader of the powerful subgroup in the church, who has now resigned, was blamed by most of the members interviewed for undermining Pastor Landis. The members of this subgroup were able to sustain their power in part because they performed many needed functions in the church. The ambivalence expressed by members was very clear: members felt reluctant to challenge inappropriate behavior because it would mean that the dissenting leaders might stop doing the work. This ambivalence and lack of ability and willingness to confront inappropriate behavior has contributed greatly to the decay of St. James Church.

There is considerable distress surrounding the fact that Pastor Landis was called for a three-year term. A lack of clarity regarding his term started his ministry with confusion, mistrust, and open conflict. A subgroup in the church, having learned of Pastor Landis's physical disability, began to speak openly about him in a very disparaging manner. The fact that there was a great degree of resistance to Pastor Landis's ministry was not shared with him directly. It took a year and a half for the degree of undermining, name-calling, and sabotaging of his ministry to become apparent to him. Some members of the council feel responsible for the loss of Pastor Landis because they did not share this information sooner.

Confusion continued until the last vote regarding Pastor Landis's continuation at St. James. The group in support (the "yes" people) regret deeply that they did not actively recruit members to come to the meeting and vote in support of the Pastor, and they accuse the powerful subgroup (the "no" people) of having brought members who are inactive in order to sway the vote. The outcome of the vote was that Pastor's call not be continued, much to his distress and that of many members.

New families who had joined the church and supported the Pastor's ministry have now left and would not take part in the Collaborative Development interviews–a situation which profoundly saddens the remaining members. They are aware that the median age of the congregation is high and that there are few families with children to give hope for future ministry.

Pastor Landis reports feeling battered by the negative spirit and the dissension. Although he is aware that this type of attacking of pastors comes from congregational dynamics, it is still personally painful and distressing to him. The report that Pastor Landis wrote for the bishop dated September 23, 1998, became a point of conflict. He wrote it in order to clarify his own perceptions of the status of St. James, as well as to inform Bishop Jameson of the church's ongoing needs.

The development of leaders did not effectively take place during Pastor Landis's ministry. He reported that enormous energy went into stabilizing the church during the first year and a half. Neighborhood children literally were breaking windows, and he was putting out metaphorical "fires" everywhere he turned. When the ministry settled down, facility decisions were made and finances brought into accountability. By then, the disruptive and negative forces seemed so great that work on leadership development was not feasible for him.

Pastor Landis reported that for his entire three year term, he received no response to his preaching but instead was met weekly with indifference to the spiritual challenges he presented. The congregational meeting of October 6, 1998, culminated in a critical split among the members when the vote did not confirm a continuation of Pastor Landis's term.

In summary, St. James Church on Ferry Avenue has for many years been riddled with divisive forces that have slowed and eventually stopped the forward motion of a mission-driven congregation. In the last few years, the congregation could not even accurately be called a chaplaincy model, as there was very little cohesion and comfort. Continued conflict between the pastor and the subgroup made it difficult, if not impossible, for genuine Christian sharing to take place. St. James is a seriously disabled, if not fatally wounded, congregation.

Present Situation

At this time, St. James could best be described as "in limbo." While there is talk of possible survival by merger, members question the reality of merging with other Lutheran churches on Ferry Avenue and question what possible product would come from that. The council was asked directly whether they felt they had the energy to provide guidance for the current members to move into the future. Each member of the council spoke to this issue; they did not individually or collectively feel they had the resources to bring St. James back to life. Many state that recovery will require bringing back the young families or finding new families; there is nothing in the church at this point to attract them. St. James reportedly has a reputation in the community for "killing pastors." Although the conversation with the council was painful (many expressed severe distress over the thought of St. James's ministry ending), there were members who felt that the closing of St. James would be the appropriate step.

There is much resentment toward the Conference at this time, both for the lack of clarity at the time Pastor Landis came and for letting the church go too far into its present state of demise without intervention. Some expressed a fear that the Conference would not support its ongoing ministry but would prefer to have the property turned over for the assets involved.

Although its leader has resigned, there is still a powerful group within the church that asserts that Pastor Landis caused the problems, that his ministry was ineffective, and that his disability made him an inappropriate candidate. The hurtful, dismissive comments made about Pastor Landis's physical disability in one focus group were at times shocking to the facilitator.

There was little indication of a desire or ability to evangelize into the community. Most of the groups were focused on blaming the pastor, the Conference, or the powerful subgroup. When each group was confronted about its own responsibility (individually and collectively as a congregation), the notion was very difficult for many to consider. The council was asked directly, "If you loved your pastor as you say you did and grieve the loss of his ministry, why did you not confront these people who you say have undermined the ministry?" The response was one of helplessness, hopelessness, and lack of power. Many noted that the people they find culpable for destroying the spirit at St. James were also those doing the work. There is a great deal of ambivalence, inertia, and lack of ownership for each person's individual part in the downfall of St. James. The church does not seem to have a core of people who have been properly trained, prepared, and empowered to lead the congregation into a healthy and wholesome future.

Analysis of Systems Issues

St. James Church on Ferry Avenue is critically wounded in its ability to move forward. There is an "in group" and an "out group," and alliances are sought through an active grapevine and telephone chain. Lobbying takes place, and sanctions are reportedly applied when members do not comply with the wishes of the powerful subgroup leaders. When the council was asked why they were unable or unwilling to put a stop to the destructive activity they observed, there was silence in the room.

As much as members of the council did not want to lose their pastor, they lacked the courage and the ability to confront the issues head on and behave in responsible ways. Some now feel guilty and experience remorse. Although most do not believe that the church is viable, some still wish to "put this behind them" and move on, in hope that a new pastor would rescue them. Neither the council nor the members felt the need for a Physis consultation, and this resistance was openly expressed.

The ability of the congregation's members to take responsibility at this time for their own contribution to the problem is minimal. Without a strong infusion of life from outside the congregation, there are insufficient resources at this time to continue ministry.

The long-standing patterns of power-brokering and competitiveness with the pastors has cost St. James greatly. The congregation at large has defaulted on its responsibility for the finances and the ongoing operations of the church by putting these functions in the hands of a few.

There is a tremendous vacuum of leadership and little understanding of the appropriate role difference between pastor and lay leaders. Each pastor throughout the history of St. James Church has met with this internal resistance, and in many cases it seems that the pastor left rather than name or confront the dissenters openly.

There is a disturbing lack of interest in spirituality and perhaps a lack of understanding of how a spiritually centered church functions. The current mission seems to be storytelling about the power struggles over the years. There is no observable Spirit-driven mission. There is still an unrealistic hope and expectation that a pastor will come along who will offer life for the future. The present members, for the most part, desire a chaplaincy model of church: they wish to be cared for, have the sick visited, and experience worship on a weekly basis. Several of the older members openly expressed the desire that St. James stay in existence so that they might be buried there.

The resentment toward the Conference is of serious concern. The church very much needs the Conference's help but feels resentful and resistant to it. While needing Conference support, some believe the Conference is only interested in their property and assets. This tension must be addressed.

Options for the Future

Merger

St. James Church on Ferry Avenue is a congregation of approximately forty worshiping members whose life together is severely threatened. The challenges that face the congregation, should it determine to move forward, are great, and the leaders are inadequately trained and empowered to carry on. Merger does not seem realistic at this time. The question needs to be asked, "What resources will St. James bring to a merger that would lead to the collective health of a larger congregation?" Power-brokering among the members is still going on. Although many report that the departure of the subgroup leader ended the problem, tension "will rear its ugly head" again when a full-time pastor is called. Competitive subgroups in churches often lose steam during times of transition, but regroup and reenter the scene when a full-time pastor is called. These times of submerged energy are often interpreted by the congregation as an end to the strife, yet one may expect such groups to continue their pattern. To bring this dynamic into a merger with other churches would not be reasonable at this time.

Closing

The closing of St. James Church is one option for consideration. The worshiping congregation is small in number, advanced in age, and has little demonstrable sense of mission. The tendency to blame others (rather than take responsibility for the current situation) is not a good sign for the future, should a new pastor be called.

Members fear the loss of financial assets. They fear the congregation's death but project the threat of congregational death onto the Conference (seeing the Conference as wanting to close them to benefit financially). There is enormous underlying grief and pain in this group that is still largely deflected by blaming.

Should this option be chosen, it is recommended that:

1. A full investigation be made of the financial assets of the congregation at current market value and complete disclosure of this information be made to the members.
2. A structured process of "letting go" be planned, which might include:
   a. A celebration of the history of St. James in the community, inviting other churches and community leaders to a time of "remembering."
   b. Discussion groups, offering members the opportunity to express feelings of loss.
   c. Educational sessions to provide insight into the dynamics of loss and death.
   d. A congregational meeting with representatives of the Conference in order for the issues of mistrust to be aired and addressed.
   e. Liturgical celebration and closing rituals that frame the past ministry at St. James positively and express the reality of ending.
3. Once this decision is reached, time lines should be established and followed strictly.

End and Restart the Ministry

If there is a mission on Ferry Avenue that might take place effectively within St. James's facility, another option is for the congregation to end the present ministry by disbanding the council and present structures. A *re-founding* process might include the following steps:

a. The congregation would turn over the facility and financial assets to others in an act of stewardship. No controls, expectations of representation in leadership, or other strings would be attached.
b. A mission-focused church in the Conference be invited to become a

mentor church, sending members who would provide a core group to infuse energy and health into the church.

c.   A spiritual core of Bible study, prayer, reflection, and spiritual teaching would be established to strengthen the faith of all, including those present members who elect to remain at St. James.

d.   When a solid, Spirit-centered congregation is established, energy would be put into evangelism. This would occur *after* internal strength is built.

e.   A minimum commitment of five years would be made to this refounding of St. James, so that all might participate without the fear that a term call would interrupt the flow of ministry.

f.   Each member of the congregation would be challenged to cooperate with refounding or to resign voluntarily.

g.   Each member would agree to hold others accountable for the goals that are set and commitments that are made.

h.   A pastor with strengths in the following areas would be called to shepherd this congregation:

1.   Personal maturity–ability to manage self well; meets own needs in personal life and not through the office of the pastor; sustains strong concept of self while empowering others.

2.   Professional maturity–a Spirit-filled, seasoned pastor with experience in troubled human systems who is able to discern and confront evil as it erupts in congregations and to hold others accountable.

3.   Profound ability to listen and understand the perspectives of those who are unable to minister while not being distracted or disempowered by them.

4.   The ability to celebrate slow movement, which necessitates patience, vision, and honoring of small steps towards health.

5.   Willingness to engage in an active program of mentoring, ongoing personal growth, and outside review of the process to maximize clarity and objectivity.

Unfinished Business

Whatever the decision is made at St. James Church, it is recommended that consideration be given to reconciliation with Pastor Donald Landis. It is incumbent upon the Council to acknowledge their abdication of responsibility and, if there is a genuine sense of the council's impact, to offer to him their apology and ask for his forgiveness.

This report and recommendations are offered with the hope that St. James Church will be led by the Spirit into a decision that will further the Kingdom of God and heal the brokenness it now faces.

Sandra Fox O'Hara
Leadership Consultant

Used with permission of Sandra Fox O'Hara, Physis Associates, Westchester, Pennsylvania.

$\mathcal{W}$elcome to the work of Alban Institute...
the leading publisher and congregational resource organization for clergy and laity today.

Your purchase of this book means you have an interest in the kinds of information, research, consulting, networking opportunities and educational seminars that Alban Institute produces and provides. We are a non-denominational, non-profit 25-year-old membership organization dedicated to providing practical and useful support to religious congregations and those who participate in and lead them.

Alban is acknowledged as a pioneer in learning and teaching on *Conflict Management *Faith and Money *Congregational Growth and Change *Leadership Development *Mission and Planning *Clergy Recruitment and Training *Clergy Support, Self-Care and Transition *Spirituality and Faith Development *Congregational Security.

Our membership is comprised of over 8,000 clergy, lay leaders, congregations and institutions who benefit from:
   ❖ 15% discount on hundreds of Alban books
   ❖ $50 per-course tuition discount on education seminars
   ❖ Subscription to *Congregations*, the Alban journal (a $30 value)
   ❖ Access to Alban research and (soon) the "Members-Only" archival section of our web site www.alban.org

For more information on Alban membership or to be added to our catalog mailing list, call 1-800-486-1318, ext.243 or return this form.

Name and Title: _____

Congregation/Organization: _____

Address: _____

City: _____ Tel.: _____

State: _____ Zip: _____ Email: _____

BKIN

The Alban Institute
Attn: Membership Dept.
7315 Wisconsin Avenue
Suite 1250 West
Bethesda, MD 20814--3211